D0723743

PRESENTED TO

BY

ON OCCASION OF

DATE

WHAT
IS
A
MAN?

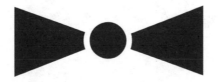

DR. JOAQUIN G. MOLINA

"This book will open the eyes of men in a way that unlocks any door that keeps them from finding their God-ordained destiny!"

Bishop Wellington Boone

Founder and Chief Prelate,
Fellowship of International Churches

Author of the popular Christian books:
I Am a Man, Not Just a Male, Your Wife Is Not Your Momma, Breaking Through, My Journey With God, The Low Road to New Heights, and Dare to Hope.

Copyright © 2013 by Dr. Joaquin G. Molina

All rights reserved. No part of this publication may be reproduced, distributed or transmitted in any form or by any means, including photocopying, recording, or other electronic or mechanical, without permission that was pre-written and the publisher's consent, except in the case of brief quotations in critical reviews and other noncommercial uses permitted by copyright law. For requests for permission, write to the publisher, addressed "Attention: Permissions Coordinator," at the address below.

What Is A Man?
P. O. Box 654338
Miami, Florida 33265
www.solmiami.org

Ordering Information:
Permission to Use Copyright
Please contact the Permissions Department if you desire to use an extract or copyright material of evidence of Dr. Joaquin G. Molina on a non-exclusive basis in book format only. Please direct your inquiry in writing to:

Spring of Life Fellowship
Attn: SOL Media Dept.
P. O. Box 654338
Miami, Florida 33265
or fax your request on official letterhead to:
(305) 597-4447

I.S.B.N.- 978-0-615-89308-2

Sales amount. Special discounts on quantity purchases by corporations, associations and others. For more information, please contact the editor at the above address.

Ordering bookstores and wholesalers U.S. trading.

Please contact the retailer:
Tel.: (305) 597-4440
Fax: (305) 597-4447
or visit www.whatisaman.com

Printed in the United States of America

TABLE OF CONTENTS

ACKNOWLEDGMENTS

I offer my deepest gratitude to my God, the Father, Son and Holy Spirit, who make all things possible and who has allowed me to communicate these thoughts and words according to His own heart.

To my Lord ansd Savior Jesus Christ who is worthy to receive glory, honor, and power for being the firstborn among many brcthrcn filling the earth with His glory.

To my world changing family, my beloved First Lady Yvette and our four wonderful children: Nicholas, Joshua, Brandon, and Christina for their continual love and support as we offer Christ our best.

To my parents, Dr. Raul G. Molina, M.D. and Julieta Molina for your love, continual help, and allowing God to use you so powerfully to raise your children up in the nurture and admonition of the Lord. Thank you for your amazing example.

To all the amazing pastors, leaders and godly men that were significant in speaking the rights words at the right times, and for modeling Christ's example. As mentors in my youth you patiently encouraged, trained and loved me through my imperfections to form my maturity in Christ-like Character.

To those co-laborers and great generals of the faith, who as faithful ministers of God, continually offer your maximum effort to serve your family and the Body of Christ as true world changing princes, salt of the earth, and light unto the nations.

A special thanks to all my spiritual sons and daughters who have faithfully joined and walk in the spiritual legacy of world-changing caliber, joined shoulder to shoulder as co-laborers in God showing the true character of Christ in your thoughts, words and actions serving their generation in God's purpose.

I also wish to speak a special blessing over all the courageous men who are willing to begin this great journey toward true manhood by obediently following the footprints of Jesus Christ and His Word thus leaving behind a great legacy and example for the following generations.

AUTHOR'S NOTE

Most men will proclaim each his own goodness,
But who can find a faithful man?
Proverbs 20:6

THE MEASURE OF MAN

The ultimate measure of a true man is not where he stands in ordinary moments of fun and entertainment but where he stands at the crossroads of life when challenged by controversy of truth, standing up for what is right. The man who chooses to courageously act with strength of integrity in the face of difficult situations and whose priority is to serve and protect the welfare of his loved ones, defending his family, against all potential harm is a true man. A true man will do anything it takes to leave a legacy of blessing to his family. He is willing to demonstrate his capacity to protect his loved ones by always standing up for what is right regardless of the fact that it may cost him to lose prestige, popularity, fame, fortunes, or any such thing that could possibly compromise the principles and convictions he holds true.

The attitude and expression of pursuing genuine manhood often results in an incredible offense taken by others, especially by those who have decided to live in the perpetual wanderings of spiritual mediocrity. Others may prefer to avoid or steer clear of this responsibility seeing the pursuit of true manhood as to difficult and choose an easier road towards a world of leisure and fantasy (non-reality) by holding on to the perpetual state of lifelong immaturity. When real life confronts these men and their unrealistic imaginations they respond with childish tantrums, full of fanciful rebellion, in a Peter Pan style, refusing to grow up. Soon all men will realize that the only pathway toward the full measure and stature of a true man is Christ and Christ alone.

Dr. Joaquin G. Molina
-World Changer

PROLOGUE

"The greatest human tragedy is not the loss of identity among the various races, nations, or religions but the difficulty in being able to identify what it is to be a real man, and I am not speaking of the loss of masculinity or a man's sexual preference but rather about his character. I hope this book can help you define the true essence of manhood for you to find true peace with God and with yourself."

-DR. RAUL G. MOLINA, M.D.
Dr. Joaquin G. Molina's Father

INTRODUCTION

This book is written for the benefit of men and women everywhere who desire to know the true meaning of what it is to be a real man. The pages that follow will help many men draw closer to the origins and essence of manhood as best explained through the greatest manual ever written about the topic; The Holy Bible. In this book, the reference to "man" is not referring to "mankind" in general, but solely to the male; and more particularly to the mature, responsible, accountable male hereinafter called "man."

In pursuit of this task, the Word of God shall serve as a reference and a conduit through its myriad of illustrations and expressions to help the reader define and describe the essence of a man. It is suggested that those who read this book take the time to follow along with the Holy Bible in hand, and meditate upon the referenced Scriptures that are quoted herein.

Our hope for those who read the following chapters is that they obtain a true understanding of the importance of man's significance and the clear depth of God's design and purpose for him. Without exception every man is called to fully know and accomplish the Creator's will. After reading this book, a person will have a firm grasp on the secrets of manhood and discover the significance of God's extravagant and lavish plan for every man's existence.

Those who lose sight of God's plan for a man will continue to withdraw and perish in the mire of hopeless despair. The resulting consequences of a lost man are so unbearably crushing that it has caused millions to suffer great irreparable pain and agony that is not easily overcome or removed. History speaks loudly of the horrible consequences suffered by all people, especially widows and orphans, who were left bereft, destitute, and robbed of the blessing of a true man who would care and protect them. Without a real man at home there can never be the awesome reality and embrace of a genuine faithful husband or a loving father.

Becoming a true man should not be left to chance, and therefore, we hope this book provides the necessary reflection and meditation to serve as a reference in helping the next generation to comprehend what is the true measure, stature, and fullness of a completely mature man. As civilization continues to progress and move forward, I believe this book will establish a precedent to help many answer the deep cry profoundly lodged within the human hearts of people everywhere that yearn for a man to arise, take his rightful place, and fill the void that is missing in this day and age.

Now, more than ever, an intense bitter cry is heard deep within the souls of all people longing for men to faithfully fulfill their call upon the earth, to serve as husbands and fathers as God has appointed them. Both women and children are yearning for men to take their rightful place and repair the damage caused by their past neglect. The greatest longings upon the earth today are children who desire for their dads to faithfully love their moms and always come home to keep and safeguard the family unit. No other desire compares or weighs heavier upon the human heart. These two cravings have impacted humanity with the most severity and will continue to have the greatest repercussions like no other for those remaining here upon the earth.

Only a real man can answer the call to manhood. If a man fails to find his genuine identity and fulfill his call it ravishes other areas of his life. For example, the absence of a man at home leaves the family without a proper anchor, losing its security, stability or support, causing the family to suffer the devastations of fatherlessness. Each time a man loses his identity and abandons his role as a husband or a father, he creates a great chasm and an emptiness left many times to be filled by an illegitimate substitute and an imposter who will never be able to represent the true substance and legitimacy of his role.

Finally, men must admit and realize that without their genuine presence and responsibility, many of the basic social structures and components of this life will continue to be severely effected; areas like, the family unit, the church community, the educational systems, entire neighborhoods, healthcare services, justice system and the many other social realms. Many lives continue to suffer enormous consequences and harm that would otherwise be eliminated and non-existent if each man was to seriously consider fulfilling his God given post and calling.

The question of why so many men have decided to abscond and become non-existent, to continue withdrawn or missing from the family is not answered herein; suffice it to say that sin has prevailed. There is no doubt that man is at the core and vital center of earth's social fabric, so without fulfilling his role and by reneging on his responsibility to attain his manhood, all other areas of life and society are severly affected and immensely suffer. Finding the answer to manhood therefore becomes the primary task for all who desire to become better acquainted and learn how to fulfill the high call, full measure, and total extent of a true man.

We can rest assured that the meaning behind manhood is not a modern enigma, contemporary dilemma or a clueless phenomenon of our day, but throughout history, human beings have always shown a continual struggle towards finding and understanding the essence of what a man is. For example, in the Old Testament book of Psalms, King David inquires as follows,

What is man, that thou art mindful of him? and the son of man, that thou visit him?

Psalm 8:4

To answer this age old question becomes our quest in the following pages.

CHAPTER I
Understanding: What is a Man?

I n all of creation's vast expanse no other being has suffered greater loss of identity than man, and as a direct result of this loss of identity, women and children everywhere consequently suffer incredible backlash. From the beginning of time the loving Creator deliberately and intentionally moved towards making man with specific precision and meticulous attention. This is recorded in the very first book of the Bible.

And God said, Let us make man in our image, after our likeness...

Genesis 1:26

It is with these very few words at the beginning of man's creation that God begins to reveal and simplify the complexity of His design for man. The core of a man's composition can reveal his identity and worth. Being made in the image and likeness of the Godhead, every man is only destined to a high purpose and great significance. In other words, God's plan for every man, as His very personal handiwork, was directed towards becoming all that would reflect the characteristics of His admirable, desirable, excellent, exemplary, attractive, outstanding, rich, majestic, noble, and faithful persona. Any thought to the contrary of this beginning becomes inconsistent, inadequate, and thus a step away from the real meaning of a man. Any departure from God's desire and heart for a man becomes a disintegration and perversion of a man's true identity. The divine attributes of God's character thus serve as a model of true manhood. Thinking, talking, and acting as God would in any given situation become the true expression of a genuine man.

With each step that a man takes away from the image and likeness of God, he automatically relinquishes his manhood and begins to immediately shrink, diminish, and subtract from his true manhood. Any and every single thought, word or action contrary to God's image and likeness becomes a distorted, disfigured, and grotesque rendition of a man. The maximum expression of true manhood is visible when a man decides to live his entire life following God's example and becoming like Him in each thought, word and action. A true man learns to follow divine patterns and principles consistent with God's presence and likeness. Among other things, God is loving, merciful, faithful, righteous, pure, holy, truthful, trustworthy, loyal, honest, humble, kind, and generous. There is no greater expression of manhood than the man who is able to think, talk, and walk evermore conveying the image and likeness of God. Therefore, the only effective way to obtain manhood is by imitating Christ. No man can recover their manhood quicker than the man who fully imitates Christ in all things. The apostle Paul confirmed this and made this his life's aim, just as he had written in the epistle to the church at Corinth.

And you should imitate me, just as I imitate Christ.
1 Corinthians 11:1

Christ is the ultimate blueprint and model for a man to follow and to imitate in order to fully express true manhood. To recover his manhood each man must follow and trace the footprints of Christ in the image and likeness of God in every expression of life. Without following Christ as the best example, each man will utterly fall short and incomplete in his attempt to portray and reflect true manhood. To develop as a man there are many diverse aspects, but the most important aspect is recognizing God's divine order in creation.

A man should never forget that from the very start of his existence, God destined him to take on God's image, according to His likeness. *(Genesis 1:26)* In other words, man was to become an exact replica of God's character. The same mind, the same words, and the same benevolence would characterize a true man. To depart from this model would cause a man to end up losing the patterns of his manhood forever.

A close look at the following verse allows all people to comprehend God's desired progression for man during his time upon the earth. Being able to thoroughly meditate and follow the flow of biblical text can lead any man to a step by step process and in this way obtain a clear grasp to a more excellent view of God's framework and design for his life. God's creational order and purpose for every man is to always lead him toward a continued path of positive and extremely favorable progression.

And God blessed man and said to him, Be fruitful, multiply, and fill the earth, and subdue it, by using all its vast resources in the service of God and man; and have dominion...

Genesis 1:28

These powerful words were spoken over the first man by his Creator on the first day of his creation and they would forever serve as the foundational words that would dictate, govern, define, and direct every man's life with every step he would be required to take upon earth.

More accurately, God's heart for every man was revealed by the seven words issuing forth from His mouth, and these words are able to reveal His sovereign desire for man. With each pronouncement, God uttered a blessing upon man and with each word there is sufficient definition to capture a deep understanding of what man is and what man is not. The words "image and likeness," "God blessed him," "be fruitful," "multiply," "fill the earth," "subdue it," and "take dominion," should all define a man's life upon the earth. Man should not take any other shape, form, or expression, nor should he submit himself to any curse, nor become sterile, unproductive, unfruitful, infertile, divisive, empty, or be overcome nor overtaken by any diversion or distraction. Rather a man should increase in productivity, be fruitful, be multiplied, fill the earth, bringing all things under his authority and responsibility, and he should govern in the realm of his dominion and within his God appointed inheritance. In other words, God created a man to be nothing less than a champion.

In order for a man to fulfill such a high call and to walk according to God's design for him to be a champion, it is first necessary to understand the sequence of God's plan. This progression can also be seen in nature's groweth process among plants that change from one growth stage to another that also follow a divine order and design.

Every plant begins with:
A.   A small seed that grows.
B.   A plant that is able to blossom.
C.   A flower that produces a fruit.
D.   A fruit that ripens unto maturity.

In the same manner, man was created to follow a specific divine order and a progression leading him to God's glorious design to fill the earth with His glory. *(Genesis1:28)*

Therefore, God created a man from the dust of the earth and destined him to have a victorious and an abundant future:

A. God makes man in His image and likeness,
B. God blesses man,
C. God commands fruitfulness over man,
D. God commands man to multiply,
E. God commands man to fill the earth,
F. Man is directed to subdue all things and finally,
G. God commands man to dominate all things by accepting responsibility over all things upon the earth that is under the domain of his leadership.

As each man repents and starts his journey back toward God's divine order, he will also find the essence of his true identity and be able to fulfill his high call to lead his family and fulfill the divine mandate as prescribed by his Maker God.

Any mindset or disposition contrary to this becomes the premise for great confusion and resulting failure. No other created being suffers like a man. Man has yet to witness a dog acting like a cat, nor do cats carry on with a dog complex. The man who allows himself to be moved to and fro in his thought life will eventually end up shipwrecked in a nefarious identity complex and ultimately reject his divine mandate to become a man according to God's design. These men who self-righteously reject God's way can often be found following after other models of manhood pursuing ungodly formulas, patterns and habits that are severely twisted leading them further astray toward the opposite spectrum of very dark perpetual wanderings.

Recently, a story was told of a certain man who rebelled from his Christian faith and decided to withdraw from a life committed to Jesus Christ as Lord and Savior. Instead, he chose steps that would cause him to renounce his manhood and decided against becoming more and more like Christ. Becoming wise in his own opinion, he began to live as an angry and immature child. In the midst of his child-like tantrums he decided to live his life according to his own selfish dictates. As a result, his life was far from Christ and he purposefully chose the well known path of rebel-lion. For many years he experienced one godless crisis after another, and after all was said and done, bitterness began to fill his wayward heart with unforgiveness, resentment, atheism, greater bouts of immaturity and more rebellion. As he continued to navigate through each of life's harsh battles his travels met with more and more adversity.

This created difficult predicaments that accumalated with increased anguish in his soul filling his life with deeper pain of regret, confusion, depression and finally horrible feel-ings of unresolved grief. In the face of despair, he decided to avail himself of a quick fix and remedy by experimenting with a certain uncoventional spiritual cure. Walking fur-ther away from God's plan, he sought relief in the ancient folklore traditions of the Amazon rain forest that promised to alleviate his tormented soul. After traveling through dif-ficult terrain to follow after the dark suggestions of meet-ing with a shaman (a witch-doctor), similar to a priest-like, potbellied indigenous medicine man to undergo the ritu-als of spiritual purification, this man found out there was no reality of inner peace or soul cleansing within the deep jungles of South America.

Rather than obeying the simple biblical principles of godly instruction, he preferred to venture out into the unconventional medicinal hallucinations under the trance-like effects of the Ayahuasca, a plant that is said to release a man's soulish torment with the promise of great spiritual purification. Once again, this portrays the attitude and example of a man who is willing to walk further away from God and take steps into a rebellious and hostile environment. Preferring to pursue the endless wanderings toward any and every other conceivable direction or spiritual path other than the time-tested truth of obeying the Bible and surrendering to Jesus Christ as Lord and Savior.

Those who are obstinate and stuck in their own ways can never find the real glorious authenticity of manhood according to God. Instead of dignity, respect, and a place of honor, immature men continue to meander towards lower forms of manhood expressing deviant behavior on the downward spiral toward shame and isolation. These men later in life try to drown their sorrows and frustrations by entertaining the lower expressions of manhood into the hellish abyss of chronic alcoholism, drug addiction, pornography, gambling, hoarding wealth, promiscuity, sexual immorality, and extraordinary pseudo-intellectualism as their preferred manner of self-medication.

The pride and arrogance that have filled the thoughts of these incipient men will continue to lead them farther and farther from God's original purpose, causing them to suffer problems with deep identity issues to the extent that they often think they were destined to a life of mediocrity and to conform to a life below the standard desired by God. For this reason they continue to seek and pursue one fantasy after another, holding on to the perpetual child-like imaginations and further postponing the inevitable harsh impact with reality which will catch up to them sooner or later. When this reality comes to the surface they will lament and realize they lost their opportunity to fulfill life's best by doing the will of God.

Just like the much celebrated case of Peter Pan, these men refuse to grow up and mature, they are totally unable to correctly respond to the challenge of true manhood. Instead, they continue to travel on their wayward journey towards "Never Land" and as a result they are unwilling to accept the responsibility for the adult life.

However, when a man decides to embrace the call to live a life of obedience, according to the instructions of God's Word, his irresponsibility, rebellion and child-like fantasies definitively disappear. At this moment, a man comes to serious terms with God, and the hope for maturity starts to reveal as his manhood begins to appear thus allowing him to finally become a great husband, exemplary father, and an extraordinary world-changing man who makes a difference wherever he goes.

There is no doubt that the majority of men have lost their way, by becoming completely and totally incompetent to show forth their true manhood and successfully partici-pate in the lives of their family members. The poor return on their familial investments and the barren crops of bro-ken hearts, broken marriages, and broken families are the only remaing fruits. Rather than finding his way and the true purpose for his existence according to God's design, today's man finds himself far from his high and noble call. Instead of finding his refuge in God to be safely kept for-ever, many man find themselves destined towards an inev-itable destruction by not keeping God's creational order. The result is that everything related to a man, including his personal life, marriage, family, children, health, business, initiatives, finances, economy, government, and civiliza-tion begins to reflect the chaos of his lost, broken, fallen condition, and bankrupt state.

In other words, since man has fallen far away from God's perfect plan and design and has decided to turn his heart toward sin and rebellion, pursuing disobedience, he inherits a life where there is a constant state of depression, disorder, and confusion in every realm of his existence. The result is anarchy and chaos, where man is surrounded by despair, agony, and affliction, perpetuating suffering as a result of his decision to live far from any fellowship with God. God's original plan for man was to result in a life that produced the fruits of peace and joy instead of sorrow. Time will forever stand still until man comes to terms with his own personal decisions to accept divine accountability and responsibility so that he will be qualified for triumph. In order to become a great leader, a man must first be willing to become a great follower, and he who refuses to discipline his character has disqualified himself to lead others toward triumph in this life.

To become a true man is a prerequisite for fulfilling God's call upon every male. But each man certified as disqualified or terminated from his vocation (divine call) the moment he refuses to grow up and mature. Any man who attempts triumph in this life without following God's true plan is pursuing a fantasy, from which he will be rudely awakened, sooner or later, to face the reality of having fallen utterly short of his true noble and significant glory. Outside of this framework, any prosperity achieved is only temporary and without any long term satisfaction and fulfillment.

Many passages within the Bible explicitly warn a man about the consequences of living a life separated from God. When a man decides to pursue an empty and deceptive dream without God, he only assures himself a reality of pain and bitterness until there is a final collapse. Ruin and tragedy are the shameful portion, every step of the way, for a man who decides to live this life in the pursuit of vanity and temporal glory.

Every man should take the time to read the exact portrait of a man's destiny that dares to defy or challenge God. This defiant man's portrait is described in Chapter 20 of the Old Testament book of Job. In a few short verses the Bible clearly describes the tragic life of any man that attempts to resist the hand of God. There is no greater description of what can befall a man who stands proudly and obstinately against God. After reading the following passage, some men will consider this portion of Scripture a self-portrait of their own lives. Take the next few minutes to carefully read this portion of biblical instruction found in Job 20:4-29. Reading these verses and taking them to heart will do a man much good to avoid many years of regret and sorrow.

"Do you not know this of old, since man was placed on earth, that the triumphing of the wicked is short, and the joy of the hypocrite is but for a moment? Though his haugh-

tiness mounts up to the heavens, and his head reaches to the clouds, yet he will perish forever like his own refuse; those who have seen him will say, 'Where is he?' He will fly away like a dream, and not be found; yes, he will be chased away like a vision of the night. The eye that saw him will see him no more, nor will his place behold him anymore. His children will seek the favor of the poor, and his hands will restore his wealth. His bones are full of his youthful vigor, but it will lie down with him in the dust. "Though evil is sweet in his mouth, And he hides it under his tongue, Though he spares it and does not forsake it, But still keeps it in his mouth, Yet his food in his stomach turns sour; It becomes cobra venom within him. He swallows down riches and vomits them up again; God casts them out of his belly. He will suck the poison of cobras; the viper's tongue will slay him. He will not see the streams, The Rivers flowing with honey and cream. He will restore that for which he labored, and will not swallow it down; from the proceeds of business He will get no enjoyment. For he has oppressed and forsaken the poor, He has violently seized a house, which he did not build "Because he knows no quietness in his heart, He will not save anything he desires. Nothing is left for him to eat; therefore his well being will not last. In his self-sufficiency he will be in distress; every hand of misery will come against him. When he is about to fill his stomach, God will cast on him the fury of His wrath, and will rain it on him while he is eating. He will flee from the iron weapon; a bronze bow will pierce him through. It is drawn, and comes out of the body; yes, the glittering point comes out of his gall. Terrors come upon him; Total darkness is reserved for his treasures. An unfanned fire will consume him; it shall go ill with him who is left in his tent. The heavens will reveal his iniquity, and the earth will rise up against him. The increase of his house will depart, and his goods will flow away in the day of His wrath."

Job 20:4-28

This portion ends with verse 29 as a horrible pronouncement, which God has prescribed as the appointed inheritance for those men who defy His ways and stand totally wayward and obstinate.

"This is a wayward man's portion from God, and the heritage appointed and prescribed to him by God."

Job 20:29

"There is a way that seems right to a man and appears straight before him, but at the end of it is the way of death."

Proverbs 14:12, Proverbs 16:25

It has never been God's intention nor His desire for a man to lose in life or to end up totally far removed from the true victory of God's plan for true prosperity and real significance in all things. In God's plan, each moment of a man's existence is designed for him to enjoy accomplishing amazing fruitful, productive, and successful endeavors in life. On the other hand, when a man forsakes God's plan he eventually suffers loss and the failure is devastating. Instead of walking toward God's game plan, he has proudly chosen to deny any acceptance of responsibility and rebelled against God to walk contrary to any godly instruction. With each initial lapse and disconnect from God, a man begins to stray from genuine success, thus resulting in his great underlying dilemma. Those who reconcile with God can heal and begin to experience a true restoration in His sovereign grace and mercy. Most human suffering can be traced to a man's wrong decision at a crucial time in life when he foregoes the call of God, and is ultimately led away from great blessing and begins the horrendous drag toward his own scheme of self-centered plans and other temporary pleasureable pursuits.

When a man decides to live according to God's instruction via the Bible, he begins to flourish and enjoy a great wealth of success, in degrees of happiness and health he never dreamed possible. A recent example of this was the biography of a legendary financial analyst who shared his personal testimony of how he fell into great financial ruin. After having enjoyed a temporary period of economic abundance and wealthy exuberance, he lost everything. He and his wife were forced to face the difficult reality of their bad financial stewardship after having lost control of their affairs and ended up losing a multi-million dollar real estate enterprise. They found themselves facing the reality of bankruptcy and suffering the awful distress of great dramatic economic devastation. After making a joint decision to steward their future income and "do all things according to God's instruction," they began to read the Bible and carefully follow the biblical principles they found. In this manner, they began to rebuild their lives by faithfully serving their new business relationships and once again enjoyed the experiencie of great prosperity in their new found opportunity. This time their season of prosperity was achieved by following the simple precepts of biblical stewardship and today they enjoy success with the long lasting principles that are accompanied by great peace. When a man learns to love God's commandments and follow precise biblical instuction he will live the reality of God's promise and experience a measure of great peace and true prosperity.

Great peace have they who love Your law; nothing shall offend them or make them stumble.

Psalm 119:165

The blessing of the Lord makes one rich, And He adds no sorrow with it.

Proverbs 10:22

The hearing of this story is truly refreshing and learning how to follow biblical instruction becomes the pathway of a new start toward happiness and success for any couple. There is no greater joy for a man than to discover, follow and apply the practical principles found within the Bible. A man who embraces and follows these time-tested priceless pearls of true wisdom can walk through life's long journey without regret. Any obstacle can be immediately overcome as a man confronts his earthly pilgrimage by following closely to biblical instruction. The Bible promises those who read and obey these principles will be filled with life-long experiences of amazing blessings accompanied with great peace and real satisfaction; this is nothing short of a marvelous and miraculous provision. All around the world there are stories of men who have found the opportunity for a new start, beginning to do things God's way, and truly follow biblical principles as a road map to life.

Another example of this reality is recorded in the Old Testament in the book of Joshua, where God invites Joshua to keep the instruction of God's Word so that he might enjoy good prosperity and find true success in all his ways.

This Book of my instruction shall not depart from your mouth, but you shall meditate in it day and night, that you may observe to do according to all that is written in it. For then you will make your way very prosperous, and then you will have great success.

Joshua 1:8

In other words, the eternal Creator extends a challenge to each man commanding them to listen and to obey His Word in order to find true prosperity. The resulting prosperity in God's promises are always "yes and amen", in all things. Every man who decides to honor God will receive a position of authority and prominence, enjoying peace and guaranteed prosperity as God's great and faithful reward.

Every biblical precept prepared for man is filled with the emphatic great and precious promises of God's blessings and great rewards. In the following passage, God continues to instruct his people to carefully heed and observe His commandments as the rite of passage to life and the very entranceway to a man's highest summit during life.

"And the Lord will make you the head and not the tail; you shall be above only, and not be beneath, if you heed the commandments of the Lord your God, which I command you today, and are careful to observe them."

Deuteronomy 28:13

God invites every man to be a true hero and a victorious champion. He desires a man nothing less than absolute notable success in all his endeavors and lifelong pursuits. Consequently, true success is determined by a man's capacity to fulfill the purpose of God during his lifetime. God is seeking men who are willing to follow Christ and change the world by restoring the order and priorities of God upon the earth just as it was in the beginning. A careful read of the New Testament book of Acts, will reveal that the first followers of Christ were known as those who were "turning the world upside down." (Acts 17:6) In other words, upon hearing the Gospel message these men were able to learn their true identity in Christ and began to live according to God's high call by refusing to follow the degenerate nature of fallen men and the broken systems of this world. These early Christian men preferred the ancient paths of God, which promise to produce true and lasting peace and tranquility over the new modern expression of manhood that only produce strife and anxiety.

"Thus says the Lord: 'Stand in the ways and see, and ask for the old paths, where the good way is, and walk in it; Then you will find rest for your souls, But they said, 'We will not walk in it.'"

Jeremiah 6:16

"The work of righteousness will be peace, And the effect of righteousness, quietness and assurance forever."

Isaiah 32:17

CHAPTER II
Jesus Christ the Perfect Model of Man

D isconnected, fallen, and wandering distant from God, man has lost his vision to comprehend or participate with the significance of his true purpose upon the earth. The state of man's wayward condition, of his endless wanderings, and constantly choosing a thousand paths to nowhere in a continued purposeless pursuit is very exhausting. From one fantasy to another, depleting his energy, and finally rendering himself tired and diminished, a man is never able to realize the true significance of his worth. Each day becomes another chapter of aimlessly roaming in the midst of temporal pleasures which always end up, time and again, at a dead end. As the need for masquerading their shameful state grows, together with their urgency to appear outwardly successful or significant, many men must reinvent their persona with each passing year to cover their true sad condition. These wayward men continually create one new façade after another, trying to hide the true reality of their emptiness, that they are totally exhausted, truly down trodden, and overwhelmed by feelings of worthless insignificance.

Only those men who surrender to God's call to fully follow and faithfully serve Jesus Christ will be able to realize a life of true significant purpose and attain the full measure of genuine joy. Therefore, if any man desires to understand the true meaning of life and to become a whole man, he should turn his attention to listen, carefully study and follow the life and footprints of Jesus Christ.

The primary reason that Jesus came to the earth was to seek and recover every lost man. Jesus is the gift of God to every man and his life the model to reestablish manhood and offer the only pathway that can lead a man to return to God's original plan. There are not many avenues that a man can travel with the promise of totally restoring his soul and which are able to address the deep needs of his true condition. In order to truly resolve the present condition of modern man's dilemma and his so-called "identity crisis," a man must seek the Lord with his whole heart for He alone has come for this purpose- to resolve this enigma and offer salvation to all men.

For the Son of Man came to seek and to save that which was lost.

Luke 19:10

As previously mentioned, man was created in the image

and likeness of God from the beginning and therefore, he can never understand the purpose of his existence outside of God. For this reason, the only way that men could ever recover their true identity, was by finding the true image of God. This was fulfilled when God sent Jesus into the world as a replica of himself; Jesus Christ is the true image of the invisible God.

Christ is the visible image of the invisible God.
Colossians 1:15

When Jesus Christ came to the earth his specific purpose was to bring men back to God. Therefore, he clearly announced, time and again, that He and He alone was the only way that man would find truth and real life. So, as a man draws nearer and nearer to Jesus and decides to become more and more like Christ, he will find his rightful place and calling as a man. These words were recorded by the beloved apostle John in his gospel writings. There in the Gospel of John 14:6, Jesus' words resound with the force of a trumpet call warning all men that unless they follow His path, learn His ways, and receive His life, they shall never draw close, nor find the Father. Through his loving words, Jesus explains how every man can come to his right senses and begin to comprehend spiritual truth, and finally begin to take meaningful steps toward God and His purpose.

I am the way, the truth and the life. No one comes to the Father except through Me.

John 14:6

If any man desires to become a true man and walk towards making a lasting difference in this world, he must be willing to follow the footprints of Jesus Christ. As the late Dr. Edwin Louis Cole, a recognized Christian author and prominent men's leader, mentioned repeatedly in his books and reminded his close followers, "Manhood and Christ-likeness are synonymous." The more a man is able to think, speak, and act like Christ, the more he can attain to the character of a true man.

Man's lack of attention in this vital area causes him to suffer and lose any sense of reality. Every man who decides to ignore Jesus Christ as the true example of manhood plunges himself into the deep darkness and great labyrinth of foolishness, and eventual mindless insanity. Only Christ can provide the perfect model to organize a man's thoughts with all clarity and only Christ's purpose can fulfill man's longing for the pursuit of happiness. The Bible clearly delineates that there is a pathway for man to obtain victory, a place where he is able to go from glory to glory, being transformed into Christ's character by the Spirit of the Lord as he faithfully beholds that image.

But we all, with unveiled face, beholding as in a mirror the glory of the Lord, are being transformed into the same image from glory to glory, just as by the Spirit of the Lord.

2 Corinthians 3:18

To distance oneself from Christ is to distance oneself from the very image of God, and this causes men to lose the essence of their character. Each step a man takes away from Christ causes his life to grow dim, becoming all the more darker and darker until deep darkness becomes a man's only reality. A man who walks away from Christ and refuses to embrace sound biblical teaching can eventually gravitate towards ridiculous speculations, including the thinking that all men originated from an evolutionary processes as derived from a lower life form or organism such as a primate (monkey), or even worse, thinking he is a god, and thus refuses to render accounts and accept responsibility before others. A man who takes purposeful steps away from God, deciding to walk far from the footprints of Christ and Christ-like character, will soon find himself losing the true sense of his identity and significance as a man. Every man who is unwillingness to continue accountable to Christ and His Lordship renders himself lost and totally surrendered to a life without purpose. All that is left for these men are the remains of perpetual wanderings through the wilderness of dry lands of confusion between one disgrace and another.

CHAPTER III
Man as Spirit, Soul, and Body

The most important aspect to consider in restoring a man back on course with his manhood is by understanding the three aspects of his person or the very basic components of his make up. The very fabric and core of a man's essence was created by God as a triune being, having a physical body, a soul, and a spirit. Men have no problem understanding the impor tance of maintaining their own *physical body* by eating, drinking, and properly exercising. In the same light, most men realize the importance of nurturing their *mind and soul* with healthy emotional sentiments. However, many men have the terrible tendency to neglect their *spirit* by living spiritually malnourished and deficient in their devotion to God. This spiritual wilderness and deprivation is the result of not being truly connected to the One who created the spirits of all men. When a man fails to responsibly nourish his spirit, he tends to wander aimlessly about in extreme unstable bouts of immaturity and expressing superficial depth in his character. Petty priorities and bad decision making seem to reveal the lack of spiritual insight and godly provision. In an attempt to cover up and disguise the lack of character, a man will try to show case his personality by exhibiting and highlighting his external accomplishments. These externals can vary widely from making cameo appearances in intellectual circles, gathering with vanity-driven acquaintances, accumulating trivial knowledge concerning world events, hoarding priceless possessions, competing in athletic events, gambling, attaining notoriety in local politics, aiming for commerical trophies, seeking temporary accolades, and by performing to achieve goal-driven quotas. These men try to find significance in talking about their latest cars, boats, and houses, what they own, where they went to school, how and where they are employed, their networth, how much money they make, what celebrity they know, and what they have or dream to accomplish in natural terms. None of these topics reveal a man's true character but are all the poor attempts to disguise a lame personality. Reality is hidden and deeply offset by the glamour of the exterior gloss as these men portray strength while, at the same time, they are hiding the true condition of their soul, which is desperately seeking for true acceptance, genuine affirmation, and unfading glory.

Prior to man being formed from the dust of the earth, God created man as a spirit being. Simply put, God is spirit and the essence of man is also spirit. Having the substance of spirit allows a man to communicate with his Maker. Who can understand or make sense of a man and of God's plans for him? Only the inner most part of man- his own spirit.

For what man knows the things of a man except the spirit of the man which is in him?

1 Corinthians 2:11

Many men will find difficulty perceiving the meaning and substance of their manhood unless they are quickened in the spirit so that their understanding is awakened. Without awakening the essential element of a man's spirit within him, no man can understand this lifelong journey to become a true man who fulfills his purpose. The descriptions of this spirit component of a man have been recorded in the earliest of biblical writings and clearly mentioned in the ancient book of Job.

*But there is a **spirit** in man: and it is the breath of God Almighty that gives him understanding.*

Job 32:8

Put another way, God communicates to every man through his spirit. Therefore every man is required to nurture his own spirit before he can follow God's instruction. Similar to the physical body of a man that can see, hear, and relate to the physical surroundings in a physical realm, so the spirit in each man has eyes to see, ears to hear, and an awareness for a man to relate to the spiritual realm of his spiritual surroundings.

This is clearly illustrated in the third chapter of the Gospel of John, when a man by the name of Nicodemus approaches Jesus at night seeking guidance. Before Jesus can respond to his questions, Jesus tells him he must be born again. This means his spirit must come alive and get in tune with God's spirit before God is able to direct any of his steps.

Jesus answered and said to him, "Most assuredly, I say to you, unless one is born again, he cannot see the kingdom of God."

John 3:3

This is not a physical birth but a spiritual birth whereby a man can begin his spiritual journey toward manhood and accept the challenge of this great calling.

Another glimpse of this is available as the apostle Paul writes to the Ephesian church praying for their spiritual health and development so that the eyes of their spirit are enlightened to know those things that pertain to their spiritual calling. As a man recovers his spiritual sight, he may walk towards the wealth and riches of his inheritance that God has prepared for him.

that the God of our Lord Jesus Christ, the Father of glory, may give to you the spirit of wisdom and revelation in the knowledge of Him, so the eyes of your understanding being enlightened; that you may know what is the hope of His calling, what are the riches of the glory of His inheritance in the saints,

Ephesians 1:17-18

A man's hope to fulfill God's purpose requires him to spiritually develop and become a strong grown up and mature spiritual being. Ultimately, each man will be truly defined by the extent he has grown and matured in his spirit. The reality every man will face is that there are always physical consequences that will follow the errors and the waywardness of his spirit. A man who is unacquainted with his obligations to nourish his spirit, whether by reason of his deliberate ignorance or his unintentional neglect, will grossly suffer during his earthly sojourn. For this reason, it necessary that all men seek to be born again, of the water and of the spirit, and know that they are ultimately peronally responsible to nourish, train, and govern their own spirit. This is the place where the Holy Bible derives its greatest importance as the nutritional source and owner's manual of a man's spiritual growth, development, and existence. The Word of God becomes the most important well spring to nourish, train, and develop a man's spirit. The Word of God is also the source of man's spiritual food, more commonly known as the "bread of life." When Christ was able to defeat Satan, during three very powerful temptations, Jesus reminded the devil that man was not to live by natural bread alone but that his livelihood would come from God's Word, as his vital spiritual nourishment.

It is written, "Man shall not live by bread alone, but by every word that proceeds from the mouth of God."

Matthew 4:4

As the apostle Peter writes in his first epistle, the Bible becomes a man's initial source of nourishment by which he is able to grow toward a healthy lifelong development to attain the desired maturity in his spirit.

As newborn babes, desire the sincere milk of God's Word, that ye may grow (mature) thereby:

1 Peter 2:2

Only when properly nurtured, does the spirit of a man grow and have the hope to attain the image and likeness of the perfect man; in the full stature, measure and fullness of Christ.

till we all come to the unity of the faith and of the knowledge of the Son of God, to a perfect man, to the measure of the stature of the fullness of Christ;

Ephesians 4:13

The writer of the book of Hebrews reminds every man that the nutritional value found in God's Word is able to sustain a man's spirit and will determine the strength of his growth and development towards maturity.

For though by this time you ought to be teachers, you need someone to teach you again the first principles of the oracles of God; and you have come to need milk and not solid food. For everyone who partakes only of milk is unskilled in the word of righteousness, for he is a babe. But solid food belongs to those who are of full age, that is, those who by reason of use have their senses exercised to discern both good and evil.

Hebrews 5:12-14

The marked difference between those who participate of milk and those who participate of solid food is determined by the capacity that they have in keeping the skills of righteousness in their spirit. As a man learns to obey the spiritual instruction of God's word and begins to exercises godliness, he will grow strong towards maturity. In the same manner, as a man becomes well nourished in God's Word, his life will show greater degrees of maturity in everything he does including the preparation to complete great works. In summary, a man's ability to grow up and develop in his spiritual maturity is determined by his discipline to thoroughly nourish his own spirit with the Word of God.

When a man steps toward this manner of growth and maturity, he will experience the true keys of successful living. The focus of true manhood is recognizing that a man's spirit within him is the starting point from which he can order and direct his steps. Every man must allow the Holy Spirit to direct his own spirit in order to understand God and eventually begin walking towards excellent wisdom and truth. Until a man's spirit connects with God's Spirit and is able to learn the way toward full maturity, he will be unable to progress any further. Men who reject this truth will fall into deep darkness and their foolish hearts will become further darkened even to the point of failing to comprehend their true identity or purpose for their existence in this life. This explanation is given to men in the book of Romans.

For although they knew God, they neither glorified him as God nor gave him thanks, but their thinking became futile and their foolish hearts were darkened. Although they claimed to be wise, they became fools.

Romans 1:21-22

When men neglect their spirit by failing to train the inner man and have become spiritually malnourished, or cannot even groom their own spirit by connecting to God and His Holy Word, they will remain ignorant concerning their existence, and thus continue to live far from the reality as God intended. These men can be considered as those who are walking in this world, spiritually disabled, suffering as lame, blind, deaf, and dumb men. In other words, these men are living without being able to fulfill the purpose for which they were created. However, when a man understands his calling, and is awakened to be alive to his spiritual responsibility before Christ, he will begin to use his spiritual legs, spiritual eyes, spiritual ears, and spiritual mouth to live for God's purpose and honor as directed by the Holy Spirit.

In the verses that follow the prophet Isaiah reminds all men that it shall no longer be the strength of a man's physical body or will that will help him survive but the supernatural giftings of the Spirit of God that are available to help men to powerfully walk upon the earth.

"There shall come forth a Rod from the stem of Jesse, And a Branch shall grow out of his roots. The Spirit of the Lord shall rest upon Him, The Spirit of wisdom and understanding, The Spirit of counsel and might, The Spirit of knowledge and of

the fear of the Lord. His delight is in the fear of the Lord, And He shall not judge by the sight of His eyes, Nor decide by the hearing of His ears;"

Isaiah 11:1-3

Every man must clearly understand that he has his own spirit, who inhabits his own physical body, in order to fulfill his divine purpose or vocation upon the earth, by following Christ as an example. Therefore, a man is supposed to join both his physical body and his own spirit to do the full will of God and accomplish His powerful bidding upon the earth.

Wherefore when Christ came into the world, he said, sacrifice and offering you did not desire, but a body you have prepared for me …Then I said, 'Here I am—it is written about me in the scroll— I have come to do your will, my God.

Hebrews 10:5, 7

Many people consider a person to have arrived at manhood when they are finally able to personally care for their own physical needs. In other words, for some people, becoming a man is measured solely upon one's ability to physically groom and financially provide for their own personal sustenance. However, reality dictates that true manhood is so much more and actually involves a person's ability to take on the full responsibility over his entire being; as a body, soul, and spirit. Therefore, full maturity in manhood is attained to the extent a man is willing to accept responsibility to properly groom, govern, and steward the matters that concern his own body, soul, and spirit, in accordance with the biblical parameters, as per the degree a man obeys God's Word.

He who is slow to anger is better than a mighty warrior, and he who rules his spirit, than he who captures a city.
Proverbs 16:32

Physical grooming and the soul's realm of emotional responsibility are only two aspects of personal responsibility. For a man to accept responsibility to guide, govern and guard his spirit before God by consistently and faithfully caring for his own inner man becomes the hallmark of a true man. There is no greater discipline for a man than to obey God's Word and stay on track on the straight and narrow path of God's pleasure, desire, and perfect will. Those who fail to nurture and groom their own spirit and continue to neglect this vital part of their life, are fast seen to fall into many sorrows and suffer great hardships and eventual ruin.

"Whoever has no rule over his own spirit is like a city broken down, without walls."
Proverbs 25:28

Great loss is the eventual consequence of those who despise taking responsibility over their own spirit. Neglecting one's own spirit causes men to pursue great fantasy and constant fleeting imaginations. Many of these men find a refreshing safe haven in the fantasy "Never Land" of pornography or the forbidden relationship of an extra-marital amorous affair where reality and responsibility are non-existent. Here is where the great majority of men upon the earth would rather congregate and thus forego accountability while they live renegade lives fleeing the realities of manhood. Those who desire to become genuine men must cultivate and groom their own spirit before it becomes unmanageable and far too late. Only when a man decides to become accountable for his thoughts, words and actions can he live towards the established purpose of God's plan which has been prepared from the beginning of time. The apostle Paul reminds the men of the Greek city of Corinth that God has furnished every man that loves Him a perfect ideal plan which has already been prepared and laid out-since the beginning of time.

But as it is written: "Eye has not seen, nor ear heard, nor have entered into the heart of man the things which God has prepared for those who love Him." But God has revealed them to us through His Spirit. For the Spirit searches all things, yes, the deep things of God. For what man knows the things of a man except the spirit of the man which is in him? Even so no

one knows the things of God except the Spirit of God.
1 Corinthians 2:9-11

This is the will of God for the life of every man, living in such a manner that every minute of every day is accounted for to fulfill God's amazing project with humanity.

Whether they admit it or not, the men who suffer the most upon the earth are those with an *"identity crisis."* These identity crisis are experienced more and more by a younger generation due to the fact that their parents have passed down this horrible curse. During the time in life when a man begins to seriously look for the answers concerning the nature of his existence upon the earth and search out for the purpose of his identity, he finds that nothing fills the void carried within his heart and his life is filled with deep saddness. It is during this time that men will generally speak out of having a lack of fulfillment or feelings of insignificance, often times requiring anti-depressants, medications, treatments or other specialized counseling. A man who fills himself with God's presence and lives according to God's plan by obeying God's Word will rarely live such a sorrowful experience. The lack of genuine significance or purpose is due to living outside of God's design, and this does not allow them to experience the true significance of who they are. Many people fail to understand that the very essence of a man's existence is spirit and the very fabric of his person is to be knitted into God's masterful plan. When man is disconnected from God's ultimate master plan, he begins to experience the sentiments of deep depression and the sinister dark weight of emotional baggage that causes his soul to suffer anguish; all this felt deep within his physical body.

In the book of Psalms, the psalmist is seen addressing his own soul (emotions) by prompting words of spirit filled encouragment in order to help carry the soul's anguish and sorrow.

Why are you cast down, O my soul? And why are you disquieted within me? Hope in God, for I shall yet praise Him For the help of His countenance.

Psalm 42:5

A man's life was designed to be spirit filled, spirit led and spirit connected, to follow God in protecting his heart and continue to live safe guarded in all the affairs of this life. The Bible often refers to this place within a man's soul as a "man's heart."

Guard your heart above all else, for it determines the course of your life.

Proverbs 4:23

A man who loses sight of this reality allows his soul to become overwhelmed to the point of affecting his ability to make good decisions. His heart and soul are flooded with the cares, worries, and anxiety, of this life; ultimately becoming side tracked and shipwrecked from any fruitful course. Instead of following God's lead many men decide to pursue the temporal passing pleasures of sin, and therefore loses sight of the eternal attributes of God's righteousness in all virtue of godliness, faith, love, peace, joy, patience, meekness, and excellence.

But you, O man of God, flee these things and pursue righteousness, godliness, faith, love, patience, gentleness.
1 Timothy 6:11

Jesus often provided the men who followed him with the godly instructions on how to return to their senses by seeking to improve their decisions and being able to follow His spiritual principles and truths. For example, in the Gospel of John, Jesus is recorded as inviting his followers to come and find the way, the truth, and the life that was connected to His heavenly Father.

Jesus said to him, "I am the way, the truth, and the life. No one comes to the Father except through Me.
John 14:6

By seeking Christ, a man could begin walking toward God and find His purpose. Simply said, if a man follows Jesus as *"the way,"* he will find the *"path to the truth,"* and this will lead a man to a measure of existence in an "abundant life," that man would not otherwise experience. While other men forego this opportunity, Jesus clearly opens his heart to announce this life of abundance for those who are humble and wise enough to choose it.

The thief does not come except to steal, and to kill, and to destroy. I have come that they may have life, and that they may have it more abundantly.

John 10:10

When a man is deficient, deprived, or immature in his spirit, then everything surrounding him reflects the brokenness of his spiritual condition. His marriage and family become only a mere reflection of the bankruptcy and the lack of virtues in his character. When a man has cultivated his spirit in great measure, then those who surround him will be able to witness the expressions of greatness. Every relationship found in a man's life, that of his parents, his siblings, his wife, his children, his friends, relatives, or co-workers, will either enjoy the experience of a healthy and wealthy essence of his spirit, or suffer the bitter heartache and frustration, of a selfish, child-like immaturity, and sorrow, due to the frailty of his own fallen and poor spirit.

The modern landscape is filled with men of little character who miserably fail in fulfilling their responsibility to their friends and loved ones. Whether it be to his fiancé in a promised engagement, to his bride in the faithful vows of marriage, or making a commitment to his children within the family and home, or even the faithful participation as a member of his church, men who cannot keep their oaths and commitments remain in small in stature. If the true character of a man is to be measured in relation to his spiritual responsibility, then every man should concern himself with the commitments they have made to lead their families in regards to growing in spiritual matters. To know God by faithful attendance at church, reading the Bible consistently, regularly praying with his family and growing spiritually closer to Jesus Christ, becomes essential to man's faithfulness to his manhood. While many men may take the initial steps to fill their mouths with very large extravagant promises and commitments, they only seem to deliver small trinkets and expressions of mediocre and inconsistent promise. They sell their big ideas and end up producing nothing in return. The theatrics of these men of very short stature seem to come right out of a fairy tale, a girl's dream come true. These men gleefully anounce and promise high hopes only to deliver ashes instead of beauty.

Definitely, huge epic personality but a small miserable character appears behind the mask of their façade. Within several days, weeks, months, and years later, their promise is broken, their commitment is canceled and the dreams of a bright tomorrow are terminated, no longer interested in fulfilling the oaths of their promises, commitments and vows; all pledges are extinguished beneath the banner of their pitiful cowardness and lack of manhood. Refusing to take personal responsibility by carrying the weight of their obligations, these little men are often experts at finding any cheap excuse to point at others, cast aspersions to blame someone else, always hiding behind others to clean up their irresponsibility. This exemplifies today's present dilema where many men showcase huge personality but carry and deliver absolutely no character. The character crisis is more clearly revealed in the many male celebrities and professional athletes who attempt to find and create their identity using "body ink," also known as, "Tattoos," without understanding that their physical bodies were created by God and deserve a higher level of honor, respect and dignity. Nonetheless, they continue to "tag" their bodies with ink and scribble of every kind and sort of doodle on their talented mortal bodies, showing reckless disregard and high contempt before God. These tattoo stained expressions of every sort show the emptiness and longing for identity that these men carry. This lack of personal restraint is another example of the world's so-called *"men"* and their present clueless state of mind to accept responsibilty to properly carry their character as an example of decency regardless of what the present godless culture dictates as fashionable.

Each day the tabloids and various media outlets are filled with wild reports of wayward men who refuse to behave themselves responsibly. More and more, men are seen as choosing to violently vent their frustations by lashing out to hurt, disrespect, and even kill those whom they owe the greatest measure of honor and deference. While men continue to make big promises to deliver excellence, they show a total inability to keep their word as expected, having children out of wedlock, breaking the oath of the marriage covenant, failing to offer any support to their wife and children and ultimately blaming others for his irresponsibility and many times even blaming the women as the responsible party at fault.

CHAPTER IV
Thoughts, Words, and Actions

The surrounding coastlines of each nation consists of many single grains of sand that have accumalated through a period of time. In the same manner, the expression of every man's complete character can be determined by the sum total of all his single thoughts, words, and actions.

It has often been said that a man's thoughts will determine his words and that a man's words will always determine his actions. It is also true that a man's actions will determine his habits, and his habits will forge his character. The reason this is so seriously important for a man to understand is because a man's character will ultimately determine his destiny. In other words, the entirety of a man's composition during his lifelong journey begins by the thoughts he allows to occupy his daily meditation and these produce the final outcome and become the fountain of man's ultimate character. When a man allows a combination of single thoughts joined together with the uninterrupted utterances of single words spoken, to become a part of his life, it will mark his life forever and eventually become the expressed and overt actions he takes.

Be not deceived; evil conversations corrupt good character.

1 Corinthians 15:33

For this reason, the *fall* of a man can be determined by the intensity of his wrongful meditation and also by the depth and substance of the evil in his thoughts, words, and actions. Similarly, the opposite is true; any man may *rise* to great prosperity through the faithful training of his godly meditation upon God's Word and begin aligning his every thought, word and action towards godly counsel.

Blessed is the man who walks not in the counsel of the ungodly, nor stands in the path of sinners, nor sits in the seat of the scornful; But his delight is in the law of the Lord, And in His law he meditates day and night. He shall be like a tree planted by the rivers of water, that brings forth its fruit in its season, whose leaf also shall not wither; and whatever he does shall prosper.

Psalm 1:1-3

When a man is able to direct his life towards godly thoughts and he decides to choose the right path, those thoughts have become the catalyst for his transformation and a brighter future. The apostle Paul writes that a man can experience a true change by being, *transformed by the renewing of his mind.* **(Romans 12:2)**

Encouraging a man to *think* differently allows him to begin *living* differently. The substance of a man's thoughts should be directed toward those things that are prescribed in God's Word. This type of meditation will lead a man to enjoy a life of abundance in God's purpose. No man can live a healthy, wealthy, and wise life unless his thoughts are honorable, organized, and well grounded. The following passage from the New Testament book to the Philippians provides a good list of limits and boundaries for a man to enjoy a healthy thought life.

Whatever things are true, whatever things are honorable, whatever things are just, whatever things are pure, whatever things are lovely, whatever things are of good report, if there is any virtue and if there is anything praiseworthy—Think on these things.

Philippians 4:8

Whatever is true, honest, just, pure, lovely, good, virtuous, and praise worthy should be the filter of every man's thought life. If a man is able to direct and control his thoughts, in a manner and consistent course that is purposeful and purely deliberate, he is actually creating his image and identity. These results are based upon the reality that as a man thinks in his heart so he will become.

For as a man thinks in his heart, so is he.

Proverbs 23:7

Thoughts are so significant because they spark a man's conscience and the conscience can lead a man toward images that guide him to a specific future that can be marvelous or cause a man to descend towards a downward spiral to a disastrous nightmarish end. If a man sets his heart toward continual fantasy and vanity becomes his preference, always deciding to pursue after temporal pleasures then he will attract all manner of immature, unrealistic desires, that are vulgar and blatantly infantile finally becoming entirely destructive in all his ways. For this reason, the Bible strictly forbids a man from making any false image.

...do not make for yourselves any false images in the form of anything, the Lord your God has forbidden this.

Deuteronomy 4:23

The thoughts permitted in a man's heart and mind also become his catalyst; more precisely, thoughts actually initiate the process in formulating the very words that a man will speak. These thoughts can begin to build a bridge toward a brighter future or lead a man to a downward a path to destruction in a fallen destiny. A man who is not careful to meditate on the proper thoughts and chooses rather to fill himself with deviant thoughts of twisted evil broodings, will also be careless with his words. We can therefore surmise that from the abundance of a man's heart come forth words, and those words coming from an irresponsible man's thought life will issue forth and usher him in a momentum toward a terrible destiny. This has been thoroughly proven through out history, that those who allow themselves to think upon deviant thoughts and make it their constant meditation to think wrong, will soon cause deviant words to pour forth from their mouths. Ultimately, these men soon birth forth and manifest the most depraved acts of intentional and unintentional expressions, living a lifelong of horribly regretted acts and holding on to a long list of lamented deeds.

When words begin to continually burst forth from a man's mouths without restraint or self-control, this initiates something that becomes a powerful force, which finally materializes into a future reality that is detestable for any person's life. Good words can catapult a man towards an amazing bright constructive future. But evil words can also become a destructive force like gangrene to human tissue that diminishes it and destroys a man towards a dark inferno of horrible proportions.

Death and life are in the power of the tongue, and those who love it will eat its fruit.

Proverbs 18:21

When a man's words lose importance and significance, his world becomes a whirlwind of total destruction; without meaning, a man's life becomes a road into deep darkness and nothing more than an unexplainable journey into further confusion. Men who have lost the ability to care and give prudence or serious attention to the words they speak will see their lives misdirected in the same manner. The state of aeronautical vertigo best describes this condition. Having lost the conscience and the sense of direction, men who journey without concern for proper words are without maturity to consider their ways or direction, and soon find themselves lost without purpose. For these men, life is nothing more than a huge blur of confusion and meaningless events that grow more and more incongruent. They endlessly ponder and wonder about the swirl of irrational circumstances and unrelated chapters. They live without any seemingly significant connection. From generation to generation these men suffer the sense of living disconnected from reality in a world where chaos reigns. Truth becomes a lie, and lies become the truth. Their "coming in" is actually a "going out," and their "rising up" becomes their "downfall."

Once again, because men are unable to govern their thoughts, they are unable to control the words that proceed from their mouths, and they become the victims of their own savvy stupidity. A true man is able to watch and curtail the foolishness of his lips, and this helps him prevent further adverse consequences later in life.

If any man offend not in word, the same is a perfect man, and able also to restrain his whole body.

James 3:2

When a man has the capacity to speak the right, wholesome, productive, and healthy words, his words become the very seeds that can bring forth a harvest of blessings, peace, and sweet fruitfulness. But, a man who speaks rashly and without the careful thought of being able to control his words becomes a fool exercising foolishness, who will soon find himself unexplicably in one ruin after another.

Those who guard their lips preserve their lives, but those who speak rashly will come to ruin.

Proverbs 13:3

Those who guard their mouths and their tongues keep themselves from calamity.

Proverbs 21:23

The well trained thoughts and the precise, wise, words of a mature man combine to provide the excellent direction for his conduct to follow. A man who has lost the ability to restrain his thoughts and properly gather his words before he speaks can be considered so reckless he eventually takes the wrongful steps of destroying every meaningful relationship in his life.

From time to time, there are news reports of large jetliner and airplanes that fall out of the sky towards a horrible crash leaving nothing but shattered debris. In order to recreate the accident scene and analyze the cause of the accident, the Federal Aviation Administration (F.A.A.) must first locate the electronic device which contains any last minute instructions sent from the air traffic control tower to the electronic systems on the aircraft. This device is more popularly referred to as the "black box," which contains the last recorded statements between the pilot and the air traffic controller. Once recovered, the authorities can accurately hear the last words communicated from the cockpit and determine contributing factors and the direct cause of the crash. Likewise, a careful analysis of a man's most recent thoughts and the words spoken right before his calamity can many times shed light to further illustrate and indicate the "why" and the "how" of the severity of his loss and the devastation of his life.

The words pouring forth from a man's heart and out of his mouth can ultimately become the driving force of his future. Learning to speak the correct words with totally precise accuracy can be compared to the small rudder that steers a large ship driven by strong winds. A good captain is able to take the helm according to the mastery of his skills to steer a large vessel towards a safe harbor. So also every man who learns how to speak wise words with totally accurate precision can obtain amazing good fruits and an abundance of great benefits according to the proper mastery of his ability.

On the other hand, the Bible warns that the opposite is also true. Those whose expertise is the gift of "godless gab" or "vain chatter" become "more and more ungodly." Drawing farther and farther away from God and His likeness, losing the essence of their original design. Reality is, if a man continues to speak words that are mere childish and tantrum driven, idle babblings, he loses and continues to subtract from his manhood. This has become a wayward man's favorite pastime, to boast, brag, grandstand, and showcase, by any means of eloquent, articulate manushia that can disguise, cover, and postpones, the present reality of his present condition. This seems to be the reason for the apostle Paul's warning to his young apprentice, Timothy, when he writes the following verses, advising him to avoid such inappropriate communication.

Avoid godless chatter, because those who indulge in it will become more and more ungodly (unlike true manhood).

Their discussions will spread like gangrene (unhealthy destruction). Among them are Hymenaeus and Philetus, who have departed from the truth (reality).

2 Timothy 2:16-18

All of a man's actions are preceded by the thoughts and the words issuing forth from the abundance of his own heart. The worst of these expressions are those that are birthed out of an attitude of pride and issuing forth to promote a sentiment of arrogance. Those men who seek their affirmation and worth on the basis of their prideful boastings can never quench the thirst in their longing heart for real affirmation and genuine acceptance.

The ancient book of Proverbs states that, "Pride is the beginning of destruction."

Pride comes before destruction, and an haughty spirit before a fall.

Proverbs 16:18

Finally, every man can rest confidently assured that his life will reflect and follow the lead and fruitfulness of his thoughts and his words. A definitely new, vast, and fruitful harvest is awaiting those who decide to move in the direction of planting good seeds in a well cultivated land. When a man carefully cultivates his life with the proper meditation of good thoughts and is willing to speak correct and meaningful words to his family, he shall reap a great harvest from which he shall enjoy amazing fruits. But, if a man should choose the reckless utterance of a fool, to speak rashly, without meaningful thoughts, based on the heated last minute argument or discussion, then he too shall stand to eat the bitter fruits of his unthoughtful, bitter, and foolish words.

Therefore they shall eat the fruit of their own way, and be filled to the full with their own devices.

Proverbs 1:31

All the deeds displayed by a man will reflect either one of two realities. A wise man will act to inherit glory and a foolish man will act to inherit shame. Those who challenge the prescribed order of God will suddenly see their future colored by glimpses of ruin they would have wished never to have tasted.

Human pride will be humbled, and human arrogance will be brought down. Only the Lord will be exalted on that day of judgment. Idols will completely disappear.

Isaiah 2:17-18

CHAPTER V
Time, Talents, and Treasures

While history has recorded the many ways that men have measured the value of their worth and existence, there are three specific standards that every man could and should utilize to determine the true priorities and direction of a man's life in order to help him govern the complex affairs upon earth. Each man has been entrusted with a certain portion of these three elements: time, talents, and treasures. As a man develops and grows in the three realms of his earthly existence, his body, soul, and spirit, training up the three aspects of his person, thoughts, words, and actions, he must finally examine the proper placement of his God given gifts, namely; his time, his talents, and his treasure. All nine aspects must be properly aligned in order for a man to achieve true success and prosperity. In the previous two chapters every man was challenged to equally address the responsibilities of his body, soul, and spirit together with his thoughts, words, and actions, but for a man to fail in accurately balancing his time, talents, and treasures may become the reason for his true downfall. The opposite is also true; when a man accurately stewards his time, talents, and treasures he can brilliantly excel and manifest the maximum expressions of prosperity showing forth excellence in all great things. A man who is pursuing wisdom should quickly realize that he occupies priceless amounts of limited time upon the earth and understanding the value of that time can become a man's best friend. History has shown that those who squandered their time and those who missed precious moments in time were never able to recover them again.

And He has made from one blood every nation of men to dwell on all the face of the earth, and has determined their pre-appointed times and the boundaries of their dwellings,
Acts 17:26

God has given each man the gift of time and this specific and certain period or season must be wisely invested to further discover and develop the talents necessary to reach and fulfill God's high call. Knowing that a man has a limited time upon the earth can help him acknowledge the urgency of seeking God with all deliberate intention. Every man's specified moment upon the earth was not to be an incidental or mistaken period of time but a purposeful and significant period. Therefore man must make most of his time to pursue and obtain wise instruction that will help him wisely build his life and not become a foolish prodigal son, who squanders his time, talents, and treasure in aimless, lost, and wasteful living.

Men must understand the usefulness of time and begin investing their time wisely. In the book of Psalms, King David prayed earnestly by requesting that God fill him with wisdom to know the limit of his days, so that he could navigate life with all purposeful intensity and with very great significance.

So teach us to number our days, that we may gain a heart of wisdom.

Psalm 90:12

Some men fail to comprehend the importance of time and seem to forget that their days upon the earth are limited in number. The value of time is not given serious consideration by these men, so they never manage to live their lives with a purposeful end in sight. A quick study of the Scriptures reveals that the men of old lived with a more accurate understanding of the times and were more acquainted with the limited measure of a man's life span. In other words, in ancient times, men, having less technology seemed to be more conscious of their time upon the earth and used it more circumspectly than their modern counter parts. In primitive times, wisemen properly scheduled their time and set aside specific periods to fulfill every necessary task according to God's planned schedule and time table. The evidence a man has matured can be seen by the manner is which he learns to value the significance of time. A mature man will always make a wise investment at every opportunity. As a man matures and obtains more wisdom, he will learn that time is extremely important because God has determined that all things are to take place within the specific order of a time and a season.

To everything there is a season, A time for every purpose under heaven:

Ecclesiastes 3:1

A true man perfects his ability to schedule and honor his time with the understanding of how preciously valuable time is for himself and others. When a man squanders his time or fails to act diligently the consequences can be non-forgiving. Many men wish they could return back to an earlier time in their life or change the date on the calender to a previous year because they were unable to take full advantage of the opportunities and appreciate the time, but this results impossible.

Another noteworthy example of how men of yesteryear diligently observed the times, is seen in the sons of a man called, Issachar, who understood the times and therefore aligned themselves to know what their nation ought to do.

of the sons of Issachar who had understanding of the times, to know what Israel ought to do...

1 Chronicles 12:32

To every man God has given a measure of time to develop His purpose. During this very specific and limited scope of time, man must refine and define his character by growing and sharpening his focus in various aspects during his earthly existence. Time is the only constant commodity that has been equally given to every man. By utilizing time wisely each man can develop his talents, making the most of every opportunity, towards a promising future. As a man improves this understanding and begins to partner with God, he will have a greater advantage to be able to develop his talents and find lasting treasure. The skillful use of time, talents, and treasure will allow a man to achieve the greatest significance and gains for the glory of God. Those men who fail to understand the importance of time, talents, and treasures will always be at the mercy of those who are more diligent.

The hand of the diligent shall bear rule: but the slothful shall be under tribute.

Proverbs 12:24

See thou a man diligent in his business? He shall stand before kings; he shall not stand before unknown men.

Proverbs 22:29

The diligence and best use of time for every man will be a key aspect to fulfilling his purpose in life. Those men that

are irresponsible in the use of their time and fail to realize the importance of redeeming that time will miss the
opportunities to develop their talents and lose as a result
of their laziness.

In addition to time, God has gifted every man with a different measure of talents that are exclusive and unique to
each man. These divine giftings are also known as talents
and are the very special expressions of God's unparalleled
characteristics so that every man may serve others in a
remarkable and uniquely noticeable manner. The talents
in a man's life have been given to him in order to serve God
and to serve other fellow humans in a particular, exclusive, and absolutely unique fashion. Regardless of the size,
measure, or quantity of these talents that a man possesses,
he is called to serve and develop his talents to the highest
measure as possible for the glory of God. If a man's talent is
to jump, he must develop his talent to jump to the highest
heights and measure as possible; if his talent is to run, he
must develop his talents to run as fast as humanly possible. Whether to build, discover, sing, or climb, a man must
refine and use his talents during his allotted time upon the
earth, to produce the most valuable treasure and present it
as genuine worship for the glory of God.

Reckoning the times and using talents wisely are very
important to any man's earthly existence. This knowledge

regarding a man's time and his being able to understand the diligent use of his talents to produce a treasure are vital to finding God's purpose under the sun. Those men who overlook the importance of the relationship between their body, soul, and spiritual function, in coordination with their thoughts, words and actions, learning to manage their God-given time, talents, and treasure, will utterly fall into a miserable emptiness and lack of satisfaction as seen in the ancient book of Ecclesiastes.

Therefore I hated life; because the work that is wrought under the sun is grievous unto me: for all is vanity and vexation of spirit.

Ecclesiastes 2:17

Everything that Solomon had failed to obtain as a man was due to the failure of getting in snyc and not being in harmony with God's assigned times and aligned with the particular seasons. Therefore, he hated life, continually suffered great loss, and wasted the efforts of all his talents, and treasures. Wisdom is so vitally important so that a man may live with the precision and accuracy to understand the time, to discover the talents, and steward the treasure so that his life does not become a whirlwind and barrage of bitterness, resentment, and unredeemable regrets.

Man's best and brightest expression upon the earth is to

live for the glory of God, utilizing his time with all wisdom, to diligently develop his talents and finally faithfully steward his treasure during his alotted lifespan upon the earth. There is no doubt that many men have diligently invested their time and wisely developed their talents to accumulate great treasure, only to discover at the end of time that they have traveled in vain seeking the wrong priorities and possessions. This is the reason why Jesus warned his followers in the following verses declaring that a man's life concerned much more than acquiring earthly possessions and knowing God was more profitable for man than gaining the whole world.

And he said unto them, Take heed, and beware of covetousness: for a man's life does not consist in the abundance of the things which he possesses.

Luke 12:15

For what will it profit a man if he gains the whole world, and loses his own soul?

Mark 8:36

There is no doubt that a man can achieve many great things upon earth by using his wisdom, might, and riches, but all these come to nothing if a man fails to understand the significance of what is truly worth while and profitable, by fulfilling his God given purpose upon the earth. Man was not created for the sole aimless futility of working day after day, plowing through life one hardship after another, suffering adversity without meaningful purpose, and carrying the deep void of insignificance. In the Scriptures, God is constantly calling every man out of his hiding place, communicating to man his worth, and telling him, time after time, to seek God's plan as man's most prized possession. Therefore, every man should make seeking God his highest priority and pursuit in life; valued as the most significant treasure upon the earth. There is no greater joy for a man upon the earth then to make his main objective the following, to know God in order to experience His eternal love by fulfilling His will and doing His pleasure upon earth.

Do not lay up for yourselves treasures on earth, where moth and rust destroy and where thieves break in and steal; but lay up for yourselves treasures in heaven, where neither moth nor rust destroys and where thieves do not break in and steal. For where your treasure is, there your heart will be also.

Matthew 6:19-21

But seek first the kingdom of God and His righteousness, and all these things shall be added to you.

Matthew 6:33

Thus says the Lord: "Let not the wise man glory in his wisdom, Let not the mighty man glory in his might, Nor let the rich man glory in his riches; But let him who glories glory in this, That he understands and knows Me, That I am the Lord, exercising loving-kindness, judgment, and righteousness in the earth. For in these I delight," says the Lord.

Jeremiah 9:23-24

The proper use of a man's time, talents, and treasure will ultimately determine not only a man's life here upon the earth, but also the rewards of his eternal destiny and future in the hereafter. For this reason, every man should truly step it up and be willing to accept the challenge to carefully watch over the proper management of his life by caring for the following nine gifts as his inventory and personal responsibility, to steward these riches according to the wealth of God's grace.

1-Body, Soul, and Spirit.
2-Thoughts, Words, and Actions.
3-Time, Talents, and Treasure.

Here is the secret of true manhood, to be able to mature, grow, and consistently live in a synchronized aligned manner in all these nine expressions of a man's life. In this manner the character of true manhood shall flourish and abound in all fruitfulness for the glory of God and as a great blessing for all people in every place.

CHAPTER VI
Faithfulness: The Cornerstone of Character

Not many people understand that there is a dying species and a nearly extinct creature in God's great creation called "a faithful man." Wherever a person travels today, the lack of truly faithful men is an alarming pandemic upon the earth. The biblical passage in the book of Proverbs also records the general tendency of a man to proclaim his goodness. Most men are willing to immediately discuss the sterling and brilliant attributes of their personality, but will never admit to be lacking the cornerstone of true character which is faithfulness.

Most men will proclaim each his own goodness, but who can find a faithful man?

Proverbs 20:6

Another translation for this wise proverb states, *"Who can find a real man?"* Many men learn to tell their "own" rendition and "personal" story by craftily declaring what they "pretend or intend to be," but their definition of what it is to be a true man is seriously distorted and skewed.

According to the Bible, a real man is he who is connected in all humility to God and "breathes" the reality of God with every breath. A true man acknowledges the certainty that he has been created by God and therefore is owned by Him. This understanding is the foundation for a man to be able to totally surrender and submit to God as Lord Almighty in order to fulfill His divine mandate. The men who rise to this great challenge of following God's divine purpose will lay the necessary foundation and cornerstone of faithfulness to be able to continue building their character of manhood.

Know that the Lord, He is God; It is He who has made us, and not we ourselves; we are His people and the sheep of His pasture.

Psalm 100:3

God is not only interested in developing a man's personality, but also his character. This has been God's desire for each and every man from the first day of his creation. The spirit of a man is manifest through the substance of his character. True character is revealed and manifested when a man is under pressure. In order to clearly see a man's character, one must see his actions and reactions when he is under the pressures of life's hardships, problems, and afflictions. During times of adversity, when difficult situations visit a man, one is able to witness the true extent and measure of his strength and the very integrity of his character.

If you faint in the day of adversity, your strength is small.
Proverbs 24:10

In order to know a man's character, one must observe his reactions under the pressures of life when the stress of difficult seasons and conflicts arise. When difficult times come to a man, his determination is tried, the strength of his character is tested, and the ability to keep his word is proven. During true hardship the character of man is shaped and revealed to prove other attributes like, courage, honor, and loyalty. Many men boast about their faithfulness and allegiance. They are quick to proclaim strength of character, the depth of moral conviction and great sincerity of thoughts, words, and actions, until the wave of adversity rises up and suddenly reveals the truth of their integrity.

For this reason, faithfulness is the authentic test and the maximum expression of real manhood. Without faithfulness, a man is without character and totally unable to offer himself to others or serve in the many other fabulous attributes that he might truly possesses. Every time faithfulness is lost it contradicts and discredits a man in all other areas of his life. An unfaithful man loses the hope of his desired goal along with the promised expectation of future rewards. A man who is unfaithful at his work is deceiving and betraying himself and his employer. A man who is unfaithful to the one he says he loves, will soon betray that love. The man who is unfaithful in his worship to God will be unable to dedicate his time, talents, and treasure with sure devotion. He will soon be removed from his place and his talents will be given to another man who will be faithful in character to produce the fruitfulness here upon earth. This is the man who will be rewarded when Christ returns again.

Placing confidence in an unfaithful man in time of trouble is like a bad tooth and a foot out of joint.

Proverbs 25:19

There are few things that are more painful than having a bad tooth or having to walk on a broken foot. These are the illustrations that have described the experience and the pain of being forced to rely upon an unfaithful man. In other words, having to trust in a man that is untrustworthy is one of life's most hurtful and bitter experiences. The souls of entire families who have suffered the excruciating ravishes, nightmares and the unquenchable anguish of deep rooted pain at the hands of an unfaithful man are best described as the unending torment, torture, and afflction of total irreparable harm. Instead of following after the image and likeness of God, to be faithful, these unfaitful man decide to follow after another image and likeness, that of Satan, hell's worst and most sinister being. An unfaithful man forever marks those who surround him with the long term scars and feelings of ruin and abandonment. His infidelity turns hope quickly into despair, and the expectations of loyalty are immediately tranformed into betrayal, causing the fire of deep seated hatred to consume the victims of his unfaithfulness from the inside out. When men are unable to deliver and faithfully accomplish their responsibility to their loved ones, the disintegration and fall out becomes totally beyond repair.

Much of the sufferings and brokenness in this present generation are directly related to the hoards of unfaithful men who have suddenly decide to abandon ship, leaving behind a war-torn disaster area of deep confusion and despair in the lives of those they have cheated. The resulting evidence of broken hearts, broken marriages, broken homes, broken lives, and broken dreams are all the rotten fruit coming from the lack of manhood and the continued unfaithfulness. This is the reason the Bible describes unfaithfulness as a serious act of treachery and deception. Therefore, unfaithfulness is considered totally inconsistent with the character of manhood and true maturity. A true man is never ever unfaithful. The aftermath which befalls and follows an unfaithful man in biblical terms is always terrible and addressed with severe and extremely serious consequences. For this reason, God will not tolerate men to continue to live in this ungodly trait nor deliver those who insist to walk unfaithfully to remain without harsh punishment and severe consequences.

The broad landscape of modern society seems to show an ever increasing number of men who choose to daily walk in a character that lacks faithfulness. In fact, the present culture seems to reward those who act with treachery and respond with cunning savviness to obtain personal advantage. However, the consequences of sin and the terrible reality of each man's separation from God's heart and His Word continues to produce effeminate men who are clueless to their call and responsibility to remain faithful in all things. However, thanks be to God that in every generation there have always been the presence of a remnant, a small group of men, who desire to please God and draw near to Him, searching and inquiring to be restored to the order of faithfulness according to God's original design for man. Faithfulness and manhood are synonymous. As a man grows to be more and more like Christ, he shows forth a faithful character that will never forsake or abandon those he has been called to keep and to care for. Men, in every generation, have marveled at the possibility of having a relationship with God and have pondered to understand this great mystery. One of these men was King David, who prayed to God as follows.

When I consider Your heavens, the work of Your fingers, The moon and the stars, which You have ordained, What is man that You are mindful of him, And the son of man that You visit him? For You have made him a little lower than the angels, and You have crowned him with glory and honor. You have made him to have dominion over the works of Your hands; You have put all things under his feet,

Psalm 8:3-6

In other words, David asked, "As I consider the marvels of your works," I ask myself, why are you so interested in man?" And the answer to this question is directly related to God's desire to entrust man with His great works. The Bible reveals that all things upon the earth were to be put under man's dominion so that he might rule over them. In summary, God ultimately desired to crown man and grant him a place of authority to have dominion over earthly affairs to serve with great honor and glory.

From the beginning of time, God always desired to entrust man with the rule over all of His earthly creation. This is why it is necessary that man, above all things, be found faithful. In this manner, God could entrust him with a greater weight of glory and have him shoulder the full weight of responsibility over the things entrusted. Faithfulness is the principle attribute of true men. If a man cannot grow in faithfulness, he will be unable to portray the true character of manhood. Faithfulness is the cornerstone and calling of the masculine character. A man cannot begin to expand his manhood until he first increases and affirms his faithfulness. The psalmist reminded every man that God's eyes are always upon the faithful, to bestow upon them the immensity of His works, and to crown them with the awesome trust of glory and honor.

My eyes shall be on the faithful of the land, That they may dwell with me; He who walks in a perfect way, He shall serve me.

Psalm 101:6

The opposite of being a man is acting like a child. Children are known to be unstable, unreliable, and inconsistent. This instability is often a result of their immaturity. In the following verse, the apostle Paul writes to the men in his letter to the Ephesians, telling them they should no longer continue to live as children.

that we should no longer be children, tossed to and fro and carried about with every wind of doctrine,

Ephesians 4:14

Whenever a man is living with instabilty, erratic movement, inconsistency, unreliability, unrest, and sudden change, he is either serving in the military or displaying immature character. This instability can be a sign of great immaturity, which is the opposite of manhood or virility. Mature men are no longer to act like children. A true man is able to make a decision and to faithfully commit to the decision he has made without displaying further contradiction. Children, however, cannot walk in this mature pattern because they are immature, indecisive, forever wavering, and constantly change their minds and steps every other minute. When a man makes a decision, the matter should be settled and resolved. The decision should carry the family even unto the next several generations.

Erratic decision making, continual employment changes, career changes, and posture changes in personal relationships and other responsibilities along with constant mood swings, are all within the purview of child-like conduct and not the healthy expressions of the appropriate behavior for a mature adult. Men must understand that those who are constantly roaming around in the shifting sands of one wilderness experience after another can never take root in any place leaving no chance for fruitfulness. Like a tumble weed in the desert, these men never grow, they never take root anywhere, they have no leaves, no flowers, no fruit, and blow from one place to another, like wandering stars from here to there, without purpose or direction.

CHAPTER VII
Godly Man or Peter Pan

In today's culture there is a social phenomenon that continues to be studied by many philosophers and sociologist who have observed an unusual trend among the male population, namely, "men that refuse to grow up." This astonishing sentiment seems to prevail among more and more men who have decided to walk contrary to God's calling and design for men to reach their full maturity. In the past, this infantile and very bizarre behavior expressed by immature men has been defined as the "Peter Pan Syndrome." This condition refers to the fictional character who decided to remain in the perpetual state of a child by refusing to grow up. Just like this fictional disney caricature, most men nowadays seem to prefer avoiding reality and would rather choose to live in the fanciful island and mindset known as, "Never Land." Men who choose to live in this "Peter Pan" inspired lifestyle and colorful fantasy world, "never" learn to face the realities of a mature life by accepting the responsibilities delegated by God. The fantasy, however, comes to an abrupt end for these men when they are suddenly faced with the haunting consequences of their irresponsibility.

In 1 Kings 1:5-6, the son of King David, Adonijah, took steps to live out his fantasy by exalting himself in total rebellion against his father and attempting to take away his throne. His fanciful intentions of violently usurping his father's kingdom upruptly came to an end. This is a prime example of the rebellious heart of an immature man who refused to accept responsability for his disrespectful actions. The Scriptures record that this man was never held accountable for his actions because King David, his father, totally refused to discipline his son, so he never learned to face the consequences of his actions.

Then Adonijah the son of Haggith exalted himself, saying, "I will be king"; and he prepared for himself chariots and horsemen, and fifty men to run before him. (And his father had not rebuked him at any time by saying, "Why have you done so?" He was also very good-looking. His mother had borne him after Absalom.)?

1 Kings 1:5-6

The apostle Paul points out that the most important step in becoming a man is the willingness to face reality and no longer live in a child-like stupor. Becoming a man requires a person to begin speaking, thinking, and acting with increased measure of maturity. Basically, a true man is one who finally is willing to make the decision to, once and for all, leave behind every childish way.

When I was a child, I spoke as a child, I understood as a child, I thought as a child but when I became a man I left behind my childish ways.

1 Corinthians 13:11

There are certain men who simply do not want to grow up and think it is very amusing to live their entire lives as a "man-child." These men open their minds to entertain every silly thought which only perpetuates an infantile mindset and they consider foolishness as their favorite sport. They continue to speak words and carry on conversations that are inconsistent with maturity and manliness. According to the Bible, they continue thinking, speaking and acting like young children.

This is nothing more than a contraction of God's heart for man. During Jesus' lifetime and minsitry, he observed this same anomaly and pointed out that the men of his generation were similar to children who refused to grow up and take responsibility.

But to what shall I liken this generation? It is like children sitting in the marketplaces and calling to their companions,

Matthew 11:16

A child-like man can never adequately address his responsibilities because he refuses to face reality. Immature men always prefer to avoid the acceptance of personal responsibility, choosing rather to live in the atmosphere of a myriad of cheap excuses and poorly articulated reasons to justify their lack of responsibility. With each justification and excuse their manhood is depleted and grows more and more irresponsible. When a child is called to confront a situation, he reacts and speaks out of fear, uncertainty, and ignorance because he is unable to see beyond the present reality. Conversely, a mature man learns to see further into the future and respond appropriately to each situation however difficult it may be. A mature man must not act out without first thinking about the consequences of his actions; he must first consider his ways and then subsequently take the next step. While it is normal for a child to instinctively react, a man should first consider all his options and afterward take the appropriate steps to wisely respond in a manner and a direction that is wise. Frequently, men are seen reacting improperly to a given situation and afterward saying, "It was not my intention," "That's not what I wanted to say," or "I did not mean to say or do that." This is not consistent with God's plan for man. The spirit of a man must be constantly connected to God's Spirit so that the man can follow God's direction in response to any given situation or circumstance.

At the end of the foregoing verse, the apostle Paul adds,

"but when I became a man I left behind my childish ways." Some men feel the need to continue expressing themselves with words and behavior that are inappropriate and childish. When these men are confronted, they look for excuses like, "I was angry and upset," or "The circumstances forced me to say this or do that," or "They provoked me to explode against my will." In reality, if the truth were known, they are acting out in a child-like tantrum as spoiled children do, showing a total lack of manhood. The normal patterns of an immature person show an inability to foresee the results of their inappropriate words and wrongful acts before they occur. Immature men, however, first speak and then are shocked and surprised by the ill effects and consequences of their words. They often act first without properly thinking and then are left to always live a continual lifetime of regrets when they are obligated to forever suffer the destructive nature of their foolish acts and premature words.

Manhood is a process which slowly progresses until maturity is arrived. The journey begins with childhood and finally concludes when a man has become a responsible adult, being able to correctly address the many challenges confronting him during his lifetime. In this journey, God makes a man first responsible for himself. What does this mean? God begins by inquiring whether a man is willing to accept responsibility, "Are you prepared to govern your own spirit?" Once again, the Bible alerts a man that is he fails to govern his own spirit, he is powerless to govern anything or anybody else.

Whoever has no rule over his own spirit Is like a city broken down, without walls.

Proverbs 25:28

In a broken down city without walls there is no protection, no provision, and no purpose. Similarly, the fitness gyms are jammed packed with men who devote endless hours to take care of their physical bodies and are able to obtain the fruit of well developed, strong, muscles through their exercise and hard work. But because these men do not rule over their own spirit with the same intensity and passion, they are coming apart at the seams in every other area of their lives; including their friendships and marriages. If these men were cities, they would be considered uninhabitable ruins. These men are able to use their talents and abilities to advance certain aspects of their lives but remain miserable failures by neglecting the most important aspect of their lives, their own spirit. The following questions must be correctly answered by a man as he begins the process of perfecting his manhood.

What are you doing for your spirit? .... Nothing.
Are you being neglectful of your spirit? .... Yes.

Is your spirit being poisoned? .... Yes.
Are you governing your spirit well? .... No.

If these are the answers given by men to the foregoing questions then they have betrayed their manhood. In this scenario, men will become the expression of a broken city without walls falling into continual utter chaos, soon to be plundered, completely ruined, and stripped of all dignity and honor. Everything God has bestowed upon these men will be violently taken away, not by an act of God, but as a consequence of their own personal irresponsibility and childish ways.

When a man is born again in Christ, God gives him the rights and the inheritance of a firstborn for the purpose of reaching maturity, and afterward, he can faithfully steward that inheritance to help others. The problem is that instead of becoming mature and wisely preserving the inheritance for the next generation, some men begin to act like irresponsible children and lose the wealth of their blessings that were to pass down to others. Upon refusing to grow up and deciding to accept their own responsibility, many men are betraying their destiny and forsaking the privilege of reaching the high purpose and supreme call of God for their lives.

Nonetheless, once a man is able to properly govern his

own spirit, God will then entrust him to another spirit so that he can care for a wife and nourish her spirit in all godly maturity and faithful character. This marital union will require a man willing to accept further responsibility and a greater measure of maturity in order to enjoy their marriage as real men. However, when a man decides to continue dragging the traumatic experiences of his youth and early childhood dilemas, he renders himself unable to effectively govern his spirit and consequently he is unfit to care for his own marriage relationship. Marriage is not the place for an irresponsible, child-like, man who constantly throws tantrums or displays the immature expressions of an under developed spiritual man. Those who walk in this immature mindset will see their wives begin to act like a mother and make it her custom to patronize the husband as if he were her small child. These continual motherly reprimands and the parental corrections of a wife nagging the husband will destroy the unity and harmony of the marriage.

In the following verse, God's reveals the scope of His plan for marriage which man should clearly follow.

Therefore a man shall leave his father and mother and be joined to his wife, and they shall become one flesh.

Genesis 2:24

This calling for men to be entrusted with another person's spirit, to be responsible for it and cultivate it, nourish and care for it, requires a man to have stability, maturity, and the necessary strength to always move forward despite any contrary adversity. The ability to take a step forward does not depend upon the circumstances, but solely becomes a question of character. The marital union was not intended as the place where men continue to act out like immature children, but for those men who decide to accept the challenge to deny themselves entirely and begin to walk in a higher degree of maturity.

The calling of God for every mature man is to be joined to his wife and become one spirit. When this is a reality, then the marital union becomes a true reflection of the unity between Christ and the Church. Ultimately, the step into the marriage union is a call for a man to walk unto the greatest expression of maturity. Many men have the tendency to steer clear away from any thought of the marriage commitment and prefer to forego this challenge and responsibility to grow up and care for a wife. Today, the night clubs are full of immature men who are willing to meet, dance, sleep around, and even date many women as long as the relationship does not call for the eventual serious long-term commitment of a conyugal realtionship. Very seldom will a man take the voluntary sacrificial steps of true love towards maturity by deciding to accept the responsibility to be entrusted to the care of a lawful wed-ded wife in the holy bond of marriage covenant before God and witnesses.

Today, men would rather pursue a "Playboy" or "Player" mentality. In other words, they prefer making everything in life, especially women, as if it were a joke or a sport to engage in foolish games or play. This drive for selfish per-sonal pleasure leads men to engage in all sort of harmful and crooked realtionships to fulfill the lust of their youth and fill their carnal appetite on every emotional fantasy, fetish and illusions by joining losely and temporarily with multiple women but never having the capacity of being faithful to any one. Even the "Playboy" icon indicates the inference "boys at play" instead of "men at work." Today's wayward men are considered the "Playboy" generation as they continue to repeat the following two things that should not charcaterize men.

1- They play.
2- They act like boys.

God desires that every man be seriously respectful, honor-able, and willing to accept the responsibility of his calling to be a man. Even though this is contrary to what today's culture is producing, this has not changed God's plan for man. The twenty-first century man is concerned about satisfying his own selfish pleasures and desires, looking to satiate his own lusts and cravings, trying to satisfy his own sensual needs. He says, "I just want to be with her, hold her hand, embrace her in my arms for a while but without having to commit to any serious relationship." No! This is not right! A true man would first defend her honor and preserve her dignity by leading her before God to safe-guard the integrity of her character with a relationship that honors God. Afterward the two can follow godly counsel and enter into the oath of a covenant marriage sacrificially loving one another before the church body showing they are willing to lay down their life for each other, but the reality is that until he can do this, an immature man is not ready to hold anybody's hand.

In the season of a man's life, when he is mature enough to be entrusted with his wife's spirit, he is called a husband. The day a man stands before the church altar in order to accept the responsibility for loving and caring for his wife, the couple will be called the bride and the groom. The word, "groom" has been defined as "one who is able to protect and make more attractive." This is better known as the art of cultivating; one who is able to care for a garden. The groom must have learned the disciplines of a gardener and be able to pull out the weeds and keep the pests out of his garden. A groom has learned through his maturity to know the art of cultivating a healthy relationship so that everything is made more precious and attractive. His future calling and his efforts as an excellent husband cause the garden to flourish and grow until the flowers blossom giving forth an abundant and continual amount of sweet fruit. A faithful groom becomes a true and fruitful husband who will make conditions perfect in his relationship in order to bear much fruit, that will increase toward great prosperity until he receives a plentiful harvest. His garden is found in his wife's spirit and soul.

When a man fails to exercise the art of marital grooming and diminishes in his skill to provide proper husbandry then his land will evidence this inability by failing to produce an attractive and plentiful harvest. Instead the marriage realtionship becomes a ravished dry and desolate wilderness where there are no flowers and no sweet fruit to enjoy having lost all attractiveness. Dry withered thorns, thistles, and tumble weeds are the only prospects. This quickly becomes a barren land that is noticeably unkept and uncultivated. This is the very sad condition of many marriages today.

In marriage, a man is required to care for the needs of two spirits, his own and his wife's. It is expected in marriage that a man nourish both, not only attending to the physical body, but the spiritual one as well. Many men hide behind their job saying, "All I do is work to pay for the bills." But women, who are essentially spiritual beings, not only have physical needs, they also require to be spiritually nourished with gracious words, heartfelt understanding, prayer, and discernment. Men should live with their wives by giving them honor, and in so doing, God will honor them in return. Many men are ignorant and fail to understand that their lack of prosperity and success is due to not having honored their wife. Their prayers before God and their blessings to prosper are being held back due to their harsh and indifferent treatment toward their wife.

Husbands, likewise, dwell with them with understanding, giving honor to the wife, as to the weaker vessel, and as being heirs together of the grace of life, that your prayers may not be hindered.

I Peter 3:7

So far, the progression toward manhood requires a man to understand childhood, manhood, marriage, and finally becoming great fathers. Fatherhood is truly an admirable and honorable phase in a man's character development. The previous step of marriage is the place for a wife to receive honor from a man and now a man must be willing to step it up toward another amazing level and challenge. By becoming a father, a man is taking another step toward accepting more responsibility and that is to care for his young child's spirit. A father is one who leaves a great blessing of legacy and identity for his offspring by nuturing and raising them up with all honor and faithfulness. If a man fails to adequately mature and does not provide the necessary honorable legacy and identity for his children according to their needs, the result shall be shameful. In fact, as the children grow up, they begin to determine and assess whether their father has been a good husband or a negligent one. The awareness of their value and self esteem comes from their father's faithful work and the children become part of the harvest. The Bible emphasizes that the parents are a child's glory.

... And the glory of children are their parents.

Proverbs 17:6b

When a man is unable to preserve and maintain family unity, the children lose the brightness of their countenance. This is the reason why so many adolescent children suffer from great depression and are seen to have a dark and fallen appearance. If children were given an opportunity to freely express themselves, they would admit their deep desire for a home where they could say "My dad loves my mom." This is the key to a child's heart and to his true happiness. When a man fails to mature and does not provide a safe haven for the needs of his children, then his children will carry shame instead of glory. Depending on a man's capacity or incapacity to be a good husband and father, his children will react in one of two ways: they will rejoice and say, "I want to be just like my dad," or they will rebel and say, "I never want to see my dad again."

Small children can be immature, but not fathers. Fathers must maintain their dignity and their faithfulness correcting their children with love and without cursing them.

The Bible says that the one who withholds correction curses his child.

He who spares the rod hates his son, But he who loves him disciplines him promptly.
Proverbs 13:24

During this period of time, a man is able to further develop his character so that his children become additional spirits that have been entrusted to his care. A man cannot poison or malnourish his children without being responsible for their destruction. Frequently, the newscast shows parents who neglect their children and eventually take a very sick child to the hospital only to find out that the child has a severe condition of malnutrition. The parents can be criminally charged, arrested, and imprisoned as a result of their neglect because they did not properly provide the care for their child's health. This example refers to the natural side of a child's life, how much more important is it for parents to care for their child's spiritual health and development.

for if a man does not know how to rule his own house, how will he take care of the church of God?

1 Timothy 3:5

A man who is unable to care for his own children cannot be entrusted with greater responsibility. A man's house becomes the training ground for every other responsibility because as a man governs his home, so it will be in other areas. It is a father's responsibility to encourage his children, not to make them bitter, but to encourage and strengthen their walk in the Lord instead of debilitating, discouraging or making them weaker.

The building blocks of manhood will grow step by step as a man, firstly, overcomes the challenges with accepting the responsibility of his own spirit, secondly, when he is entrusted with the responsibility to care for his wife's spirit and thirdly, when he is entrusted with the responsibility over his children's spirit, and fourthly and lastly, when he is entrusted to a ministry, where he is ultimately responsible to serve and care for the spiritual condition of the many souls who are at church or in a particular mission field. There are men who desire to become ministers of the gospel, but do not understand that this requires an incredible amount of the acceptance of great responsibility that includes, serious faithfulness, stability, wisdom, understanding and most of all maturity. To participate in any ministry, a man must be willing to allow God to train him up and endow him with the power to grow into all of these amazing attributes.

The apostle Paul wrote these words to his young disciple Timothy so that he could commit his ministry charge to faithful men, and this would be the key to his ultimate success.

And the things that you have heard from me among many witnesses, commit these to faithful men who will be able to teach others also.

2 Timothy 2:2

Faithfulness is *required* by God and *desired* by women and children all over the world who are crying out for, "a faithful man." Not personality, but character. Personality is temporal. Character is eternal. Personality is for a moment. Character is permanent. Men may come to church and sing "Hallelujah," but the most important issue is what they are when they return home and all the members of the church are no longer present? What they demonstrate in private is their actual character. A man's character is revealed by his interior, but his personality is revealed by his exterior. I pray that men everywhere can understand that God has called every man to this amazing journey to be prepared by God's Spirit to be found approved, faithful, and victorious in their manhood and not to inherit the shameful folly that befalls the unfaithful and immature.

The wise man shall inherit glory, But shame shall be the legacy of foolish men.

Proverbs 3:35

Finally, there is only one way to explain the process on how God intends to transform every man in every place so that they are able to manifest the likeness of a true mature man. The explanation is by following Jesus' example, who was willing to accept the full weight of responsibility and lived totally faithful to His Father by watching over His own spirit. In this manner, he also accepted the full responsibility for the spiritual condition of the whole world including his family, friends, and His Church.

Through the Holy Spirit, Jesus offered himself up and accepted the responsibility from his Father to provide salvation for the spirits of all men. In the same manner, faithful men work hard to show themselves approved by first having been faithful in watching over their own spirit and becoming the great leaders in their homes by serving their families and ruling well. Afterward, they can accept the responsibility to carry the weight for other areas such as caring for the church and nations of the world. Anyone who desires to become a faithful man must begin to move his life in the direction of God's original plan. In this way,

God can eventually entrust him to care for all those things placed under his dominion, and finally make him a ruler over all the works of His hands. God's righteous standard is that those who are faithful over the small things will soon be entrusted over a greater measure so that they can be entrusted to larger responsibilities.

His lord said to him, 'Well done, good and faithful servant; you have been faithful over a few things, I will make you ruler over many things. Enter into the joy of your lord.'

Matthew 25:23

Every man must remember that from the beginning of time, God made man in His image and according to His likeness to fulfill God's perferct plan. Therefore, the Bible reveals this image and likeness as follows:
"Christ is the image of the invisible God."

Colossians 1:15

If the first man was originally created in the image and likeness of God, then, every man has the high calling to live like Jesus Christ and grow upward until he reaches the stature, measure, and fullness of Christ, as a perfect man. A true man is not required to speak eloquent words, but rather, he should limit himself to speak those words which Christ would speak. Likewise, the steps of a man may not take him very far, but they should always be aligned with the footprints of Christ. A true man's marriage should be a reflection of Christ and the Church; every man is to love his wife as Christ loves the Church; to cherish and nurture her always and in all things, and even if necessary, to be willing to die and give his own life for her.

The glory of God upon the earth will be manifest when faithful men arise to follow Christ towards the full expression of true maturity in their manhood. When this occurs all the families of the earth will proclaim Jesus Christ as Lord and King of Glory, and the Church can reveal itself as the true sons of God by ultimately manifesting God's glory upon the earth. A world-changing man will cultivate, develop, and mature in his spirit, leaving behind all child-like thoughts, words, and actions, thus abandoning what is carnal and temporal in order to reach forward toward the mark of true maturity. A true man will desire to reflect the genuine maturity of manhood, as he lives upon the earth, by walking in the understanding of God's plan and being able to live, think, talk, and act with all deliberate wisdom, showing himself to be the true measure of Christ's character in all things.

CHAPTER VIII
Finally a Man

As previously stated, Christ is the perfect model of a true man and his life was able to change the world. Historically, there has not existed a more excellent model for a man to follow as an example of true manhood but Jesus Christ. Only Jesus, through the power of the Holy Spirit, can show a man the way to maturity; therefore, every man should desire and permit Christ to grow within their lives because He alone is the hope of man's glory.

To them God willed to make known what are the riches of the glory of this mystery among the Gentiles: which is Christ in you, the hope of glory.

Colossians 1:27

Other men who have accepted this challenge to become like Christ refused to quit or surrender their efforts until Christ was formed in their own lives. This reality of becoming like Christ became the apostle Paul's lifelong passion. This is evidenced in the following verse written to the Galatian church, where Paul refused to rest until

Christ was formed into the lives of those he taught.

My little children, for whom I labor in birth again until Christ is formed in you!

Galatians 4:19

The secret of how to become a true man, one who can change the world, is revealed in the life of Jesus Christ. By carefully studying the Holy Bible, a man can discover the secret pathway and the amazing powerful progression of becoming a man after God's heart. The following verses of the well known messianic passage in the book of Isaiah can provide every man with a character outline to become a great man according to the purpose of God. The different aspects of character development observed in this Old Testament passage provide a clear trajectory for those men who desire to seriously change the world. The prophet Isaiah writes the following words that foretell the coming of the greatest man who has ever lived upon planet Earth.

For unto us a Child is born, Unto us a Son is given; And the government will be upon His shoulder. And His name will be called Wonderful, Counselor, Mighty God, Everlasting Father, Prince of Peace. Of the increase of His government and peace There will be no end, Upon the throne of David and over His kingdom, To order it and establish it with judgment and justice From that time forward, even forever. The zeal of the Lord of hosts will perform this.

Isaiah 9:6-7

Men need not look for any other model of manhood because herein God carefully reveals the exact progression for a man to be able to reach his full manhood potential by simply following the footprints of Jesus Christ. The first step in this progression toward manhood begins with the glorious reality that all men were designed to be born of God as children and subsequently grow up to fulfill their great destiny as excellent and exemplary men.

1. *"For unto us a child is born."*- There is no argument that every "male" is born and begins his journey as a child to develop in maturity with all purposeful deliberate intention. Being a "male" is determined at the moment of birth, but being a "man" comes only through the process of maturity. Childhood is a totally natural and normal step in the development of every man. All men begin as a "child," but eventually, they must grow up, mature, and learn to take responsibility to fulfill and accomplish the remaining steps toward maturity. As previously mentioned, the apostle Paul wrote to the Corinthian church explaining his journey through the childhood experience as a necessary step in this progression to be like Christ.

When I was a child, I spoke as a child, I understood as a child, I thought as a child; but when I became a man, I put away childish things.

1 Corinthians 13:11

When a man fails to grow up and put away his childish things, he becomes a dangerous predicament and soon his immature character wreaks havoc becoming an embarrassment and social chaos for all those in relationship with him. Perpetual childhood is a curse for every nations. This predicament and curse has been recorded from ancient times in the proverbs and writings of wise kings.

Woe to you, O land, when your king is a child, And your princes feast in the morning!

Ecclesiastes 10:16

Men who refuse to mature are a disgrace and an abomination to those around them. These immature men will be unable to sustain a stable marriage and their family will suffer loss because they do not have the capacity to assume the necessary responsibilities to lead well. A man like this is undisciplined and cannot harness his emotions with the necessary restraint to wisely guide his home or other responsibilities. A man who continues to remain in the state of childish immaturity by desiring to prolong his boyhood years and refuses to grow up, must also perpetuate his fantasy world. In other words, he is never able to co-exist with reality, and therefore when he grows up, he cannot cope with real life responsibilities. This syndrome is known worldwide as the "Peter Pan Syndrome." The legacy of these men is a reproach to their sons and daughters who ultimately are forced to carry the humiliating backlash and shameful weight of contempt due to their father's wayward character.

2. *"Unto us a Son is given."*- During this next step of maturity God decided that a "child" would grow up and enter into another period, where he is ready to become a "son." When he is a small "child," a boy is generally closer to his mother, but when the male child begins to grow up, he begins to relate more often with a father figure. A "child" passes from his mother's care and nurture to the paternal tutelage of a father figure in order to learn how to become a "son" by perfecting and learning obedience under the father's authority and discipline. Both stern admonition and correction are an essential part of the father-son relationship. Within this framework of love, trust, and protection a son can be led into a fully developed and mature man, who is able to reach the maximum expression of his manhood.

Train up a child in the way he should go, and when he is old he will not depart from it.

Proverbs 22:6

Without the necessary dynamics of this relationship with a father figure, who is willing to consistently train him, a man will never be able to adequately develop his character completely towards full maturity. This process of perfecting a son's character through discipline and correction helps him to learn obedience. The hardships and suffering of a father's proper correction can lead a son to grow up, become a good son, and arrive unharmed to enjoy his manhood. Again, the footprints of Jesus Christ serve as the perfect example of a son willing to suffer the hardship of discipline to learn obedience and attain full maturity.

though He was a Son, yet He learned obedience by the things which He suffered.

Hebrews 5:8

Even Christ was willing to learn obedience by trusting the father in this manner. Those who avoid being corrected by their father figure and resist the necessary disciplines and admonitions for their bad conduct will never be able to reach the true standard of being a good son. Those men who skip this process of character development can never successfully attain to their calling as mature man. When a man is able to properly reason and maturely direct his thoughts, words, and actions in a correct manner this tend to be the measure and the stature of his manhood. That is the reason that a father must correct his child thorugh proper discipline to train him up as a faithful son in order that he may obtain the perfect measure of maturity as a true man. As the author of Hebrews writes,

if you endure chastening, God deals with you as with sons; for what son is there whom a father does not chasten? But if you are without chastening, of which all have become par- takers, then you are illegitimate and not sons.

Hebrews 12:7-8

Through this process of discipline and correction a man is blessed to learn obedience. When a man is able to align himself with obedience, it will carry him always to the excellence of character so he could successfully accom- plish the fulfillment and the weight of his responsibilities. This is a necessary process so that later in life a man can be entrusted to faithfully carry the full burdens of all his assignments in the diverse areas of his life. This explains why the Word of God insists that a son honor his father and mother so he can receive the promises of a long life filled with blessings and the prosperity in all things.

Children, obey your parents in the Lord, for this is right. 'Honor your father and mother,' which is the first command- ment with promise: "that it may be well with you and you may live long on the earth.

Ephesians 6:1-3

Both, a man's prosperity and his future success, depend on his development as a good son. For a man, being able to confront any future conflict in life will depend on how well he learned obedience to follow the footprints left by those fathers who taught him during his adolescence. A man's capacity to successfully carry other future responsibilities in life is determined by the measure of his obedience as a faithful son. Those men who were rebellious during this period will always lament during the rest of their days for not having endured the proper disciplines nor having learned obedience. Without discipline and correction a man cannot responsibly govern his spirit and therefore he must relinquishes his responsibility to others. This refusal to accept responsibility for his own actions renders a man shipwrecked to remain in the youthful character of a perpetual child that continually suffers the fruits of his inability to properly control his wayward thoughts, words, and actions.

3. *"The government will be upon His shoulders."*- The next step in this process for a man to continue climbing upward to become a true man is accepting the challenge to carry the serious weight of responsibility this life has to offer. After a man is trained up as an "obedient son," his father will begin to entrust him with various tasks. During the time a son is entrusted with the various tasks and weights of responsibility and he is able to faithfully obey his father's

instructions, he will begin to display unique talents and abilities which will reveal his leadership capacity. It is this weight of that responsibility upon a son's shoulder that determines the seriousness of his manhood. The weight of responsibility a son is entrusted with will give him the worth and the valor of his courage and the very measure of his manhood.

In today's culture, young boys are seen everywhere who refuse to accept any weight of responsibility from their fathers and prefer to spend endless hours joining with their wandering peers who offer no direction and refuse to accept commitment of any kind. However, those young men who are willing to accept their father's instructions and faithfully carry the weight of responsibility using their God given talents will be recognized as men of courage and honor. This will allow them to carry a good name that will precede future prosperity and good success. Every man shall be known by the measure of his faithfulness, honor and courage. A man who is double-minded is also unstable and therefore incapable of carrying any weight of responsibility; this man is always learning and never able to come to the knowledge of truth. Reaching true manhood means a man has learned the importance of his ability to faithfully carry weighty matters upon his shoulders and accept full responsibilty for the same. This faithfulness in different tasks and other delegated responsibilities marks a man and demonstrates the essence of Christ-like character. In other words, a man receives his name and leadership potential in the measure and proportion to the character he manifests. A man's potential prosperity will seriously depend on how faithfully he has learned to carry those responsibilities entrusted upon his shoulders. Accepting responsibility within the principles of honor, respect, integrity, and perseverence allows a man to successfully endure the future weight of increased glory. In other words, a man's prestige, position, and power will increase according to the weight of the responsibility he can faithfully assume. A man's faithful character qualifies him to reach beyond the ordinary to the extraordinary so that he can continue to glorify God in greater expressions of his manhood.

4. *"His name shall be called Wonderful."* - During this step a child who was born and allows himself to be disciplined and corrected by a father figure, and subsequently, passes through the training of the father/son relationship to receive a certain weight of responsibility, is now prepared to receive a good name.

A good name is to be chosen rather than great riches, Loving favor rather than silver and gold.

Proverbs 22:1

It is here during this step that a man is ready to find a wife and enter into to the lawful and sacred state of Holy Matrimony entering into the covenant oath of marriage.

Therefore a man shall leave his father and mother and be joined to his wife, and they shall become one flesh.

Genesis 2:24

He who finds a wife finds a good thing, And obtains favor from the Lord.

Proverbs 18:22

As a man successfully transitions through the learning phase of an apprentice, he is now ready to take on greater weight of responsibility in marriage relationship. The desire to establish his own family coupled together with his willingness to give his word in an oath of covenant of marriage is the true evidence that he has become a mature man. The Bible records the apostle James as writing,

For we all stumble in many things but if anyone does not stumble in word, he is a perfect man, able also to bridle the whole body.

James 3:2

The maturity of a man is demonstrated in his capacity to keep his word. Here the evidence of his true manhood is established by his commitment to love, care, protect, and provide for his own wife and family. A man will never be able to attain the purpose of God until he unites with his wife to demonstrate to the world how Christ loves the Church. In that same example, men are to love and care for their own wife as Christ loves the church. The covering a man provides for a wife by giving her his "surname" more commonly known as a "last name," and willing to lay down his life for her in order that he might present her as a glorious bride not having spot or wrinkle or any such thing, but that she should be holy and without blemish before the Lord. This is how a man can truly affirmed his maturity and manhood.

5. *"Counselor, Mighty God, Everlasting Father, Prince of Peace"*- If a man can grow up through this process and fulfill the ultimate expression of his manhood, then God will allow him to continue the process of maturity until he becomes a wise and knowledgeable man, filled with all the full measure of the manifold grace of God. A true man will continue to grow in this maturity until he becomes a "father." During fatherhood a man is required to accept even greater responsibility to guide, guard, and govern his children as the ultimate protector, provider and parent. A man's greatest challenge and responsibility is to reproduce, having his offspring and being willing to raise, form, teach, and perfect, as good obedient children that will one day become good husbands, great fathers, and heroic leaders.

These mature men will rise up to become a father to their own biological children and to also raise spiritual sons and daughters. These men will fulfill God's desire for a man to be fruitful, multiply, and fill the earth by bring many sons to glory. A true man who has reached maturity will be able to tell others what the apostle Paul told the Corinthian church in the following verse.

Imitate me, just as I also imitate Christ.

1 Corinthians 11:1

How precious to know that a man can achieve God's calling to become like Christ. This is not a mere intellectual exposition, nor a religious exercise of philosophical rhetoric, but a call towards perfecting one's character by each day becoming more and more like Christ.

What a glorious calling of God, for lost, sinful and and confused males to have the opportunity to begin a process of transformation. Growing each day according to the image of an obedient son who enjoys to walk before his Eternal Father toward the high call of maturity. The reality for every true man according to God's heart is to be able to faithfully serve the world as a mature man, in the true meaning of manhood. Every day is a challenge for a man to become a better husband to his wife, a champion father to his children, a blessing to his family, a faithful member of his church and a patriarch to the nations. This is God's pattern, to raise up true men as obedient sons, as was the case of Joseph, the prince of Egypt, who became a great man and a recognized figure at the end of his life as "the father to Pharaoh."

So now it was not you who sent me here, but God; and He has made me a father to Pharaoh, and lord of all his house, and a ruler throughout all the land of Egypt.

Genesis 45:8

6. "Of the increase of His government and peace there will be no end."- This portion of Scripture reveals that the progression of maturity in every man is an ongoing process. Not that any man has already attained the fulness of maturity, but as the apostle Paul writes to the Philippian church that a man must continue pressing forward.

Brethren, I do not count myself to have apprehended; but one thing I do, forgetting those things which are behind and reaching forward to those things which are ahead.

Philippians 3:13

During this final step of a man's development towards maturity, God will continue to entrust him with further priviledge of spiritual authority and anointing to lead the nations. God has designed man to become a great prince and leader to lead all nations, tribes, and tongues in the spiritual worship and faithfulness to honor God as supreme King of Glory. Since the beginning of time, God formed man to walk before Him as a perfect being. The psalmist wrote the following words,

For you have made him a little lower than the angels, And you have crowned him with glory and honor.

Psalm 8:5

Sadly, very few men will ever experience the great splendor, glory, and honor of being crowned by God's favor. Those men who are faithful to answer the high call of accepting the responsibility to serve their generation in the will of God with a vision of changing the world will receive such reward. In this manner, God's glory can cover the earth as the waters cover the seas.

CHAPTER IX
Love vs. Self

Lastly, a man can either confirm or deny his manhood depending on how well he is able to express love. The essence of Christ is love. If Christ were to be defined by any one word it would definitely be the word "love." In the same way, the highest calling for any man is to live in the full expression and embodiment of God's love. When a man can express this love toward others, in every direction, at all times, and regardless of any possible setback or circumstance, he has arrived at the full character of Christ. God created man so that he could respond with love and continue to grow toward a greater capacity to love others. When a man understands this reality, he will make every opportunity, in all his relationships and situations, to improve his character to love others. In this manner, every man could begin to live each day learning more and more how to express and communicate God's love in the most meaningful, sincere and profound way; showing enormous maturity.

There is no greater joy for a man than to participate in healthy relationships, and this becomes one of his greatest pleasures and also one of man's greatest challenges to confirm his manhood. For this reason, a man's family, church, community, city, and nation becomes a platform for him to develop in the expression of love, showing forth true manhood. More particularly, when a man participates in a well-balanced atmosphere, in the measure of the width, length, depth and height of Christ's love, then he will be reflecting the full embodiment of God's image and likeness. For this reason, the apostle Paul reminds the Ephesian church, in the following verse, that they must learn that God's call to every man requires them to be well rooted and grounded in the love of Christ.

that Christ may dwell in your hearts through faith; that you, being rooted and grounded in love may be able to comprehend with all the saints what is the width and length and depth and height— to know the love of Christ which passes knowledge; that you may be filled with all the fullness of God.
Ephesians 3: 17-19

Outside of Christ's love there is no hope for any man. Every now and then, Christ will require a man to demonstrate sacrificial love so that man might have the opportunity to experience true life. God's divine plan for every man is that he would be willing to grow in love towards God and continue to grow in love towards others. This love feast becomes the most generous, splendid and extravagant manner of life to live as a true man upon the earth. During Jesus lifetime upon the earth, whenever any man confronted Him with a question regarding his motives, he responded by pointing to love as the pathway to man's every victory. In the following verse, Jesus points a lawyer to the love path.

Then one of them, a lawyer, asked Him a question, testing Him, and saying, "Teacher, which is the greatest command- ment in the law? Jesus said to him, "'you shall love the Lord your God with all your heart, with all your soul, and with all your mind.' This is the first and great commandment. And the second is like it: 'You shall love your neighbor as your self.' On these two commandments hang all the Law and the Prophets."

Matthew 22:35-40

Time and again Christ directs every man to take the high road of love. In other words, if a man desires to live an abundant, true, full, and high measure of life upon the earth, he must decide to obey God's greatest command- ment. By developing a real capacity to truly love, first God and secondly others, a man will experience the most amazing, exuberant, and satisfied life ever. To be able to offer genuine love to others becomes the true measure of maturity in men and therefore, authentically loving others, marks the true standard of real manhood.

Love is the perfect expression of denying oneself. In other words, once a man learns how to love, he can begin to deny the essence of "self" and beome totally free to express his manhood to the highest level. If reflecting the image of Christ reveals true manhood, then every man should walk as Christ did, denying himself on every possible opportunity. Therefore, it is correct to say, a true man is measured by his capacity to love. When a man fails to grow up toward full maturity, he cannot demonstrate love and his whole life becomes a horrid series of selfish expressions and the continual pursuit of personal ambition at the expense of others.

The opposite of love is selfishness. Ultimately, the essence of a man's prosperity is based on the depth and significance of his relationship in two specific areas. This is the reason a man's attention should focus upon loving God and loving others has his highest priority upon the earth. There can be no lasting and true prosperity for man without relating to others in a significant and mutually reciprocal manner. The powerful weight of selfishness in a man's soul will lead him to eventually destroy every relationship in his life. A man who decides to live selfishly will see his family and friends withdraw and become unable to withstand the difficulties and conflicts created by his totally narcissistic, self absorbed, and egotistical character. This is the reason the Bible warns men not to be selfish. Those men who have decide to live selfishly and at the expense of others will eventually end up totally isolated and alone. Man was never created to live the horrible consequences nor the unfruitful dark effects of a selfish lifestyle. Those men who depart from God's plan soon witness their life becoming a total hellish nightmare where their selfishness creates an atmosphere where demons and ruins are the only final fruit. God never intended for any man to live totally excluded, isolated and far removed from others. Some men are decieved into living lonely lives as a result of embracing more and more selfish attitudes. Their refusal to love or serve anyone but themselves is a curse. Many times, men think that their selfish attitudes are justified because they are avoiding getting hurt by others. This is nothing more than a lie.

The most dangerous human upon the earth is a selfish man because his motivation is to continually move in the direction of his own personal interest, seeking the sole desire of his heart, and satisfying his lust, at the expense of others regardless of the price. Most of the criminal acts, vile expressions, and depraved acts of men, including the many psychiatric and mental disorders that exist today began with a seed of selfishness. The endless expressions of mental illness including psychological disorders, manic depression, demented thoughts, bipolar, schizophrenia, anxiety attacks, and other tormenting conditions are cultivated by the sick minds of pleasure-seeking, reckless, and self-centered people.

"For where envy and self-seeking exist, confusion and every evil thing are there."

James 3:16

While the immature man continues to seek his own pleasure, the symptoms of his irresponsibility, unfaithfulness, immaturity, wrong attitudes, and his proud, know-it-all disposition begins to surface and destroy any and every possibility he has to enjoy any healthy and genuine relationship with others. The man who continues to sow the seeds of his own selfish, personal interest stands only to harvest a crop of isolation and loneliness. Both isolation and loneliness can be categorized as the unfruitful results of selfishness and they both stand totally contrary to the expression of love.

A man who seeks his own desire willfully separates and estranges himself breaking out against all wise and sound judgment.

Proverbs 18:1

Compassion, which is derived from the Latin word cumpassio, (with passion, literally means "to suffer together," "to share in suffering or pain") and empathy in Greek, "empatheia," ("moved, excited"), are the capacity to be able to feel what someone else is feeling. Both are human feelings and sentiments that are manifested during someone else's suffering, which show one's cognitive capacity to perceive in a common context what another person is feeling. More intense than empathy, is compassion. Compassion goes further to understand the emotional state, pain, and need of another, and it is accompanied by the desire to alleviate or reduce that person's suffering, offering assistance and help. Opposites of compassion and empathy are "cruelty," "inhumanness," and "insensitivity."

God is a divine being full of compassion and empathy for humanity, and this compassion is manifested not only through a feeling of affection, but through His intervention and participation in man's reality meeting his needs, comforting him, and helping man carry his burdens. These two virtues of character come out of love and are the foundations upon which families, churches, cities, and nations are built along with a desire to join others with the same traits.

The difference between a mature man and an immature man is revealed at the moment in which one shows forth the aforementioned virtues, provoking emotions that motivate him to act. When a man shows the inability to have compassion and empathy for others in his family or social circle in a given moment of need or affliction, it is because he has closed his heart to love and is giving a place to act selfishly and immature, even if he justifies his indifferences with many excuses.

For this reason, it can be inferred that compassion and empathy are only possible in an individual capable of reasoning and examining himself first, one who can evaluate his own sentiments toward others in a way that does not seek his own interests or desires. The prevailing desire to please oneself and ignore the responsibility to act with compassion and empathy is the cause of human degeneration and thought, and it is the beginning of a mind without virtue, more or less, depending on the depth of recognition of one's own selfishness and willingness to share in the needs of others.

In everyday life, the essence of love that a man is called to express, must be accompanied by these two character virtues. The attitude of being able to completely surrender before someone else's need, omitting the desire to express one's own worries, feelings, and thoughts in order to offer another person one's own undivided attention. This involves offering a quality relationship, founded on attentive listening, in which one concentrates on understanding the feelings and fundamental needs of the other person as a priority. People who have empathy and compassion are those capable of listening to others, understanding their problems and motivations. For this reason, people who serve the interest of others usually possess a high social recognition, having made themselves aware of others' needs, even before their peers are conscious of them, and they know how to identify and make the best of these opportunities to render assistance. A true man offers and demonstrates love toward others by constantly pouring out his life to embrace the needs, hurts, and pains of those around him as a normal code of honor and way of life.

Furthermore, this capability of showing compassion is susceptible to development and growth according to the measure that men exercise and practice the same. The maturity to show compassion is increased more easily by those who have not necessarily had similar problems nor endured hardship, but were rather, men who were raised by parents or enjoyed family structures that cared for them during childhood and lived in an atmosphere of acceptance and understanding, having received comfort during times of sadness or fears, and have seen an example and model of caring for others. In actuality, when emotional needs have been cared for and addressed since the early years of life, it later allows a person to demonstrate a greater awareness and capacity to understand the needs, sentiments, and feelings of others that are suffering hardship by being able to comprehend and by placing themselves in the shoes of others and correctly responding to their emotional needs.

In this manner, manifesting compassion and empathy also demonstrates the intellectual capability of a man that has a healthy and sound mind, seen by the expression of good behavior and excellent decision-making. In extreme cases, today, more and more, children suffer from illnesses such as autism, Asperger's syndrome, and other serious psychological conditions with a common denominator of a greater emotional disconnect or a decreased ability to display or cognitively respond with appropriate feelings of empathy or compassion; but on the contrary, those who are called to maturity in manhood will exercise great awareness characterized by the ample development of compassion and the ability to love. Studies have shown that this capacity to demonstrate love and compassion is usually most observed in parents, probably due to the fact that having one's own children and caring for them is so innate within the human heart.

The apostle Paul states that the mark of a true man will be undoubtedly confirmed in someone having the real capacity to "rejoice with those that rejoice, and weep with those that weep."

that there should be no schism in the body, but that the members should have the same care for one another. And if one member suffers, all the members suffer with it; or if one member is honored, all the members rejoice with it.

1Corinthians 12:25-26

When a man is able to embrace the virtues of compassion and empathy, he will begin to share and take part in the joys and the sadness of others. Many times, compassion has been relegated and associated only to feelings of sorrow towards those suffering or passive sentiments of pity for victims; however, compassion is much more than that. Showing active solidarity, a positive attitude of generosity, and undergirding the needs of others by participating in tangible expressions of thoughtful acts of compassion are extremely important for those aspiring to be like Christ. Having the compassion to serve others, demonstrate love, and meeting their needs are necessary as this results in being seen as incomprehensible if it were not for God's love expressed through the hearts of men. This was the example set by Jesus Christ and it will serve as a great model for true men to follow. In the following verse Christ continues to set the bar at a high standard of maturity by giving another example for those men who desire to express true compassion and love.

Greater love has no one than this, than to lay down one's life for his friends.

John 15:13

The opposite of manhood is infancy. The center of a child's universe is himself, constantly offering his alliance to the horrible trilogy of "me, myself and I" which are the permanent expressions of child-like men. Without love there can be no hope of manhood. To ever reach the level of true manhood it is first necessary for a man to deny himself. Jesus Christ is the true example of manhood because He decided to love, first and foremost, and then lay down His life at the cross for all men.

A man's capacity to love is like climbing a mountain, taking the necessary steps upward toward higher and higher elevated degrees of maturity. When a man is able to deny himself and lay down his life for others, he will be empowered with the great freedom to constantly love those who surround him. There is no greater expression of manhood than to die to "self" so that a life of unselfishness love can begin to flourish in our relationships with others.

A man full of self-centered ways and personal ambitions has no time for anyone else but himself. Therefore, he cannot make himself available to generously serve and love others. An ambitious man's unbridled cravings and rampantly reckless desire for more and more in every direction begins to destroy his personal relationships with family and friends, cheating himself by taking his very own dignity. This self-absorbed, self-determined go-getter, suddenly and unknowingly turns into a distorted monster becoming all the more, inconsiderate, sensual, lust-filled, greedy, unkind, thoughtless, insensitive, uncaring, hard-hearted, ogre, and tyrant lives in an expression totally contrary to manhood. The image the world has of the courageous and magnanimous hero and victorious champion is most visibly tangible in the life of Jesus Christ, who denied himself and died upon the cross for love's sake. This is the reason that manhood can only be defined and exist through the expressed virtue of Christ's love. When a man is courageous enough to love strongly and passionately, by serving God and others, his manhood is visibly present and properly represented. When a man refuses to love, he is displaying cowardly character and betraying the proof of his manhood.

Love allows a man to deny himself and show the proper compassion, concern, and care for the necessities and interests of others who surround him.

The apostle Paul warned the believers in the city of Corinth to stand firm and act valiantly as strong men with all bravery according to their capacity to show love in everything they did.

Watch therefore, stand firm in the faith; be brave men, be strong; let all your things be done in love.
                                                  1 Corinthians 16:13-14

The apostle Paul communicates to the Corinthians through

the foregoing verse telling the men to stand firm in faith as brave and courageous men, and this is only possible when all things are done and motivated by love. The power of love equips men with the courage to respond and confront any predicament known to man. Love serves as the greatest fuel for fulfilling the call to manhood. Each relationship that is established during the journey of a man's life requires a greater capacity to love. Each day requires a man to show forth more and more courage, and this requires a man to deny himself more and more by taking up the cross of Christ and crucifying his selfish interests as the necessary step to act as a true man. To leave behind the selfishness that accompanies the single life is necessary to become a husband, and after enjoying the marriage life as a spouse it is further required and necessary to deny yourself even more to offer oneself to children and become an excellent father.

On each occasion man must decide to surrender all things and tell God "not my will but thy will be done, Oh Lord," and this becomes an opportunity to arrive at a greater degree of manhood. Many a man, however, choose not to love because they consider it a loss of personal time, a giving from the heart and a sacrifice of personal involvement. These men would rather not share their love and time with anyone because caring for others becomes a messy, unpredictable and unmanageable quagmire. An unloving man is immature and chooses to live his life motivated by his selfish mantra of pride, better known as the art of self preservation of the me, myself, and I personal complex.

The short description of love that follows can help men align their character to God's heart. As a man learns to walk in this love as described by the apostle Paul, he will destroy the immature expressions of a self-centered life that contradicts true manhood.

"Love suffers long and is kind; love does not envy; love does not parade itself, is not puffed up; does not behave rudely, does not seek its own, is not provoked, thinks no evil; does not rejoice in iniquity, but rejoices in the truth; bears all things, believes all things, hopes all things, endures all things. Love never fails."

1 Corinthians 13:4-8

A true man is willing to follow Christ on the highest path of love, knowing that love is a more excellent way. The magnitude, importance, and value of a man in the kingdom of God will depend on his capacity to love with "agape love" which is the love of God.

Though I speak with the tongues of men and of angels, but have not love, I have become sounding brass or a clanging cymbal. And though I have the gift of prophecy, and understand all mysteries and all knowledge, and though I have all faith, so that I could remove mountains, but have not love, I am nothing.

1 Corinthians 13:1-2

CONCLUSION

For the man who desires to make a difference and change the world, there is one last piece of advice so that he may always be encouraged and never give up. In the book of Proverbs, God's Word warns man to always seek and gather with wise men, for this will make him wiser. Also men are to avoid the company of fools, for this will lead them sooner or later to experience destruction.

"He who walks with wise men will be wise, But the companion of fools will be destroyed."

Proverbs 13:20

Every man ought to know that the opposite of "destruction" is "instruction" and therefore, be willing to carefully observe godly counsel to avoid the irreparable ruins during his lifetime. God's promise found in the book of Psalms has the key to becoming a blessed, prosperous, and flourishing man who remains far from ruin and calamity. This involves "not walking in the counsel of the ungodly, nor standing in the path of sinners, nor sitting in the seat of mockers" because no one who does so ever prospers. The advice of ungodly, sinful, arrogant and proud men cannot help a man change the world.

Blessed is the man who does not walk in the counsel of the ungodly, nor stands in the path of sinners, nor sits in the seat of the scornful.

Psalm 1:1

The apostle Paul also warns men that their character stands to undergo metamorphosis at serious degrees depending on who they draw close with.

Do not be so deceived and misled, wrong companionships, communion, and associations corrupt and deprave good manners, morals, and character.

1Corinthians 15:33

There is no doubt that God the Father, the Son, and the Holy Spirit can fill a man with such amazing wisdom, grace, power, and mercy to follow in the example of Christ until he reaches the goal of the upward high call. Every man on this world-changing journey must place his confidence on knowing that God will fulfill His purpose and plan with each and every man that loves Him.

"For whom He foreknew, He also predestined to be conformed to the image of His Son, that He might be the firstborn among many brethren."

Romans 8:29

Men should never lose heart and always be confident, without doubting, as the apostle Paul writes to the Philippians, that Christ will finish His work in us.

being confident of this very thing, that He who has begun a good work in you will complete it until the day of Jesus Christ;

Philippians 1:6

FINAL PRAYER

My God and eternal Father, you formed me from the beginning to be a man; your work is perfect and your purpose is eternal. From my mother's womb you knew me, and I was separated since that time to do your will. I praise, magnify and glorify you as the King of heaven because all your works are true and your ways are just; I offer you endless and continual thanks for your grace and mercy.

Forgive me for having wasted so much time in perpetual wanderings distant from your will for my life. I pray that I may always walk in your ways and that you restore my character according to your designs in each of my thoughts, words and actions.

Today, I present myself before you with all my spirit, soul and body, to devote my time, talents, and treasures, as a sweet pleasant offering and fragrant aroma of a life that seeks to please you always in all things. I also pray that your amazing grace and your eternal love will show me the way and join me as I purpose to give you all the glory, honor, and power. One day I will come before your throne of Glory and see you face to face, just as you are, and I will be like you. Until then, I want to be an example for my generation of what manhood is according to your heart.

DECLARATION OF MANHOOD

"I _____ , declare today that
YOUR NAME HERE

I accept full responsibility for my life, and I will make my decisions based on a sound moral and obedient judgment according to God's Word. I acknowledge that God has given me His Word, His spirit, and His grace, and these are sufficient to guide me in taking my next steps. I am an integral part of His Church, and His authority keeps my back at all times. I renounce and refuse to blame others for my errors and mistakes, forgetting those things which are behind and reaching forward to those things which are ahead, responding to the high calling of God, to be a true man in all fullness of maturity, in the name of Jesus Christ.

To Schedule:
Retreats, Conferences or Events:
www.whatisaman.com

Tel.: (305) 597-4440
Fax: (305) 597-4447

What is a Man?

P.O. Box 654338
Miami, Florida 33265
jmolina@solmiami.org
www.solmiami.org

NOTES

NOTES